Confederate Women

Confederate Women

Bell Irvin Wiley

Contributions in American History, Number 38

GREENWOOD PRESS

Westport, Connecticut • London, England

Library of Congress Cataloging in Publication Data

Wiley, Bell Irvin, 1906-
  Confederate women.

  (Contributions in American history, no. 38)
  Bibliography: p.
  1.   Chesnut, Mary Boykin (Miller) 1823-1886.
2.   Clay-Clopton, Virginia, 1825-1915.   3.   Davis,
Varina (Howell) 1826-1906.   4.   Women in the Confederate
States of America.   I.   Title.
E467.W48   973.7'13'0922 [B]   74-5995
ISBN 0-8371-7534-8

Library of Congress Catalog Card Number: 74-5995
ISBN: 0-8371-7534-8
ISBN: 0-8371-8357-X   Paperback edition
First published in 1975
Second printing 1975
Paperback edition 1975

Greenwood Press, a division of Williamhouse-Regency Inc.
51 Riverside Avenue, Westport, Connecticut 06880

Manufactured in the United States of America

To Andrew David Holt,
*fellow Tennessean, distinguished educator,
and long-time friend*

and

*to the memory of Fredonia Abernathy Bass,
my beloved grandmother who, during my youth,
told me many stories about her Confederate girlhood
in Middle Tennessee. She loved God and most
of his children—Yankees excepted.*

Contents

Illustrations

Introduction

Women of the South played an important role in the bid for Southern independence. During the heightening of sectional tension in the 1850s, wives and daughters of Southern leaders encouraged their menfolk to resist "Northern aggression." When the Republicans triumphed in the presidential campaign of 1860, those living in the lower South came out strongly for secession; after the attack on Fort Sumter in April 1861, and Lincoln's call for troops, women of the upper South added their voices to the chorus of disunion. With the outbreak of hostilities, women of all areas and classes urged the males of their families to offer their services for defense of the homeland. Departure of the soldiers for theaters of war caused a flood of weeping, but as a rule tears were shed in private, after public demonstrations of enthusiastic support for the war-bound recruits.

While the men were mobilizing for conflict, the women zealously turned to the making of uniforms and accouterments for friends and loved ones in the army. As the war progressed, women, like the men, lost much of their martial ardor. But for the most part they remained firm in their support of the Southern cause until the last year of the war; even after defeat became a certainty, some continued to urge unrelenting resistance to their hated foes.

Throughout the conflict women played a leading role in providing a livelihood for themselves and their families and in supporting the military effort. Some upper class ladies took over the supervision of plantations. Others sponsored soldier-aid activities and administered relief programs for needy civilians. Women of all classes found employment in the factories that sprang up throughout the Confederacy for the making of munitions, clothing, and other commodities required by the fighting forces. Some women became nurses and hospital aides; others worked in government offices. Wives, mothers, and daughters of the nonslaveholding yeomanry, by far the largest segment of Southern society, plowed the fields, cut the firewood, slaughtered the hogs, nursed the sick, and buried the dead, while their husbands, fathers, and sons, too far away to render assistance and comfort, provided moral support.

The chapters comprising this volume were first presented in December 1971 as a series of lectures at the University of Tennessee, honoring Andrew David Holt, President Emeritus of that institution. The subjects of the first three chapters—Mary Chesnut, Virginia Clay, and Varina Davis—were selected for several reasons. First, they were members of the South's ruling elite in both the antebellum and Confederate periods; second, they were in Washington together as wives of United States senators on the eve of the Civil War and later in Richmond as spouses of high-placed Confederate officials; third, they left abundant records of their experiences and impressions, in the form of diaries, letters, and reminiscences; and fourth, they represented distinct types of Confederate womanhood: Mrs. Chesnut, the childless intellectual; Mrs. Clay, the inveterate Southern belle; and Mrs. Davis, First Lady, wife, and mother. The fourth essay attempts to portray the role of Southern women in general, with emphasis on the activities and attitudes of the less privileged whites and the blacks.

Women have always held more fascination for me than men, and my interest in Confederate women dates back to the many long talks I had with my maternal grandmother during my childhood days in West Tennessee. She was a teenage girl living in Middle Tennessee during the war, and after the conflict she married a young Confederate veteran. In her conversations with me during the years 1910-1924, she often reminisced about her Confederate experiences. Hers was an invaded land, and she remembered vividly the coming and going of the opposing forces; the terror created by the approach of the Federals; the shortages of food resulting from incursions of both Yanks and Rebs on chicken houses, pig pens, fields, and gardens; the resort to homespun for clothing; and the development of all sorts of improvisation to meet the needs of everyday living. She was more fortunate than some in that her family owned slaves, a portion of whom remained on her parents' farm during and after the Federal invasion and helped provide sustenance for both whites and Negroes.

My interest in Confederate women was deepened during the preparation of my doctoral dissertation at Yale in 1932-1933, treating of Southern Negroes during the Civil War. In my research for the dissertation I traveled through the South and read the letters, diaries, and memoirs of many Southern women. I learned still more of the experiences and activities of Confederate women when I did the research for *The Life of Johnny Reb* and *The Plain People of the Confederacy* in 1940-1942, for *The Road to Appomattox* in the early 1950s, and for *Embattled Confederates* in the early 1960s. Preparation of *The Life of Billy Yank*, 1948-1951, also provided some valuable information on Rebel women, especially their reactions to Federal invasion and their relationships with the men in blue. For the past several years the women of the Confederacy have been the central theme of my research activities.

During the course of my investigations I have benefited from the generous assistance of many institutions and individuals. I am especially indebted to the staffs of the Museum of the Confederacy, the North Carolina State Department of Archives and History, the Mississippi Department of Archives and History, the Tennessee State Library and Archives, the Jefferson Davis Association of Rice University, the Southern Historical Collection of the University of North Carolina Library, the South Caroliniana Library of the University of South Carolina, and the manuscripts divisions of the libraries of Duke University, the University of Alabama, the University of Georgia, Louisiana State University, and Emory University.

I am under deep obligation to Mrs. Cato Glover and Mrs. Arthur Metts of Camden, South Carolina, for their kindness in giving me permission to quote from the manuscript diary of Mary B. Chesnut on deposit at the South Caroliniana Library. In comparing the manuscript diary with the printed versions, I benefited from an unpublished term paper, "Mrs. Chesnut's Diary—A Reappraisal," written by Louise Pettus, now of Winthrop College, while she was a student at the University of South Carolina. I appreciate her generosity in making this excellent study available to me. Mrs. St. Julien R. Childs of Baltimore kindly shared with me material about Mary Chesnut gleaned from various sources, and gave me an advance copy of her biographical sketch of Mrs. Chesnut prepared for *Notable American Women* (3 volumes, Cambridge, Massachusetts, 1971). Hudson Strode, Professor Emeritus of creative writing at the University of Alabama and biographer of Jefferson Davis, graciously gave me access to the large collection of Davis manuscripts that he donated several years ago to the University of Alabama Library. Kenneth C. Cramer, Archivist of the Baker Memorial Library of Dartmouth College, kindly made available to me a xeroxed copy of the typescript used by Ben Ames Williams in preparing his 1949 edition of *A Diary from Dixie*. I am indebted to Mrs. John W. (Varina) Stewart of Santa Barbara, California, for providing portraits of her great grandparents, Jefferson and Varina Davis, made about the time of their marriage.

Historians, librarians, archivists, and other friends living along the route of my research travels provided food, drink, good fellowship, and professional advice. They are too numerous to permit individual mention, but I want them to know that I am profoundly appreciative of their hospitality and kindness.

Confederate Women

1

Mary Boykin Chesnut—
Southern Intellectual

The late Ben Ames Williams modeled the central character in *House Divided*, Cinda Dewain, after Mary Boykin Chesnut. In the preface of his 1949 edition of Mrs. Chesnut's renowned *Diary from Dixie*, Williams stated: "An afternoon with Mr. Pepys or with John Evelyn, if I could have them for the asking, would not tempt me; but I would give a good deal to listen for an afternoon to Mrs. Chesnut."[1] Elsewhere Williams referred to Mary Chesnut as "a woman with a touch of genius."[2] Other leading writers shared Williams' high estimate of Mrs. Chesnut and her diary. Douglas Southall Freeman, while criticizing the journal for "confusion and transposition of events," characterized it as "the most famous war-diary of a Southern woman."[3] Lyman Butterfield, distinguished editor of the Adams Papers, rates the Chesnut diary as "the best written by a woman in the whole range of our history . . . in the same top bracket with that of Sewall, Byrd, Cotton Mather, John and John Quincy Adams, William Bentley . . . and Sidney George Fisher." He adds: "Even in their company her book remains unique as a revelation of a woman's mind and heart; in short, a great book by a great lady."[4]

Along with the status of "a great lady" Mary Chesnut enjoys

3

the distinction of being one of the most amply portrayed women in American history. This is because of the frankness and fullness of her journal. The complete record, as Mrs. Chesnut wrote it, covers the period November 1860-August 1865 and runs to approximately 400,000 words. The first published version, which appeared in 1905, was a selection of about 150,000 words edited by Isabella Martin and Myrta Lockett Avary. The only other edition, that of Ben Ames Williams, published in 1949, is twice the length of the first. The approximately 100,000 words still unpublished are mainly poems, quotations from the diarist's readings, letters, and asides that have little or no relation to other items appearing in the record.

Some further comment on the diary is in order. Mrs. Chesnut generally recorded her experiences and impressions on a day-to-day basis. Except for portions covering the early months of the Confederacy, this was a rough record, written sometimes in telegraphic style, on poor quality "Confederate paper." After the war Mrs. Chesnut transcribed the diary, most of it in small notebooks, but some parts she rewrote on legal pads and loose sheets. Following completion of the transcription, she destroyed all the original except three volumes (and some loose pages) covering the period November 11, 1860-October 1, 1861. These three volumes, along with forty-four notebooks and fifteen pads containing the handwritten transcription, are on deposit in the South Caroliniana Library of the University of South Carolina at Columbia. I have examined these manuscripts and I have read the typescript of them which Ben Ames Williams used in preparing his 1949 edition.*

*All the quotations from the diary that follow are from Mrs. Chesnut's manuscript. Unless otherwise indicated, quotations are from the revised version, written after the war. For the period November 11, 1860-October 1, 1861, the only period for which a record definitely identifiable as an original, wartime version could be found, quotations are, with the exceptions noted, from the original.

In making the transcriptions Mrs. Chesnut did some revising; just how much cannot be known because of the destruction of most of the original. In 1883 the diarist wrote Mrs. Jefferson Davis that she had been working over her journal during the past two years and that she was planning to continue the rewriting. The principal revision made in the period covered by the three original volumes was the elimination of material telling of her brief estrangement from Mrs. Davis in the summer of 1861. This incident will be discussed later in treating the relations between the two women.

Mrs. Chesnut intended to publish the diary after completing the revision, but she died before she could do so. She bequeathed the manuscript to Miss Isabella Martin, a South Carolina teacher with whom she had developed a warm friendship during the war and who was the subject of favorable comment in the diary. In 1904, when Myrta Lockett Avary visited South Carolina to do some research on the Confederacy, Miss Martin told her about the Chesnut diary and her desire to publish it. Miss Avary was an experienced editor, with publishing connections. From her conversations with Miss Martin arrangements were made with D. Appleton and Company for publication of the Chesnut diary under the joint editorship of Misses Avary and Martin. This edition contained only a little over one-third of Mrs. Chesnut's revised narrative, and excluded some of the diarist's most critical comments about slavery, Southern society, and the Chesnut family. The editors also toned down some of Mrs. Chesnut's caustic characterizations; for example, they changed the diarist's statement that a certain woman was "as ugly as sin" to "she was not pretty."

In 1948 Ben Ames Williams, the New England novelist, was asked to prepare a fuller edition of the diary for publication. He saw the handwritten volumes, but he actually worked with a typescript prepared for him in South Carolina. From my conversations with Williams and from examination of the copy that he submitted to Houghton Mifflin Company, I know that he had complete freedom in determining what should go into his edition. I also know that his principal aim was to include everything that was historically important and to produce an easy flowing, readable narrative without changing the meaning of what Mrs. Chesnut wrote. He worked with her revised version, as Avary and Martin had done, but he had before him a verbatim copy of the three original volumes and he included some statements from them. For example, he included from the original in the entry for March 31, 1861, Mrs. Chesnut's statement about her husband: "He came home enraged and accused me of flirting with [ex-Governor] John Manning. I went to bed in disgust.* Williams also recorded from the original, with minor stylistic editing, one of the diarist's strongest condemnations of slavery and of its effects on the morals of the masters including the statement "Under slavery, we live surrounded by prostitutes . . . Like the patriarchs of old, our men live all in one house with their wives & their concubines."** The only thing that might be called "censoring" was his omission of some of the diarist's anti-Semitic remarks. For example, he deleted the following from the entry of January 22, 1864: "Saw a lovely Jew. Elsewhere Jews may be tolerated—here [in Richmond] they are the haute volee. Every body every where has their own Jewish exceptions. I have two—Mem Cohen—Agnes deLeon." In a reference to Franklin Moses, Jr., aide to Governor Francis W. Pickens of South Carolina, the diarist wrote: "Little Moses [who is] not even out of the bulrushes yet—an infant Jew." Williams struck out this as well as her statement that, while her

---

*Williams changed the date of the entry from April 1 to March 31, and did some editing. The statement as written by Mrs. Chesnut was: "April 1st . . . Mr. C came home so enraged with my staying at home he said to flirt with John Manning. Thus I went to bed in disgust. . . ."
**Mrs. Chesnut's words were: "Here we live surrounded by prostitutes . . . like the patriarchs of old our men live all in one house with their wives & their concubines."

husband rated Judah P. Benjamin very highly, "the mob only calls him Mr. Davis' pet Jew."

In his desire to make the narrative readable, Williams took liberties that no reputable historian would consider taking. He inserted transitions, supplied missing words, and corrected misspellings.* He also did some paraphrasing to achieve brevity. But he generally took great care not to do injury to the meaning that the diarist sought to convey. From the standpoint of meeting the needs, and desires, of the general reader, his was an outstanding job of editing.

What sort of person was the woman portrayed in the diary and in other extant records bearing on her colorful career? First, it should be noted that she came from a privileged background. Born on March 31, 1823, near Camden, South Carolina, and named Mary Boykin, she was the eldest child of Stephen D. and Mary Boykin Miller. Her mother's antecedents were socially prominent; her father, though of humbler origin, graduated from South Carolina College in 1808, studied law, and served successfully as congressman, governor, and United States senator. Mary Boykin Miller received excellent schooling at private institutions in Camden and Charleston, where she acquired notable proficiency in French, German, literature, and history. Her precocity is evidenced by a charming letter she wrote to her senator father shortly before her ninth birthday, telling him that she was looking forward to reading his recent speech on the tariff.

While attending Madame Talvande's School in Charleston,

---

*Once, at least, Williams apparently took over briefly as diarist. Mrs. Chesnut concludes "Book 47," the last volume of her revision, with a letter of August 1865 from Isabella Martin, which closes with the statement: "Your last letters have been of the meagerest. What is the matter?" Beneath this statement on the final page of the typescript, in Williams' hand, appears the words: "What is the matter? Enough! I will write no more."

thirteen-year-old Mary met James Chesnut, Jr., of Mulberry Plantation, near Camden, twenty-one-year-old son of one of the richest
planters in South Carolina. The young man, a recent graduate of
Princeton, then reading law in the office of James L. Petigru, must
have been much attracted to the sprightly girl, for the acquaintance
soon ripened into romance and three years later the couple became
engaged. Shortly after the betrothal, Chesnut sailed for Europe for
a period of study and travel. Just before leaving Charleston he
wrote Mary: ''Ah, dear girl, you know not how much I love you. If
I could breathe my whole soul into a single word I would tell you.''
Six weeks later he wrote from Paris: ''I feel the happiness and
distinction of being loved by you, and I will endeavour so far as in
[me] lies to become worthy of the girl I love and honor. There are
no hopes that stir my soul, no visions bright . . . which amuse my
fancy that are not colored with thoughts of you . . . your smiles,
your approbation, your happiness would be far sweeter than success itself, and success when shared by you would be the earthly
happiness to fill my soul. . . . Your letters, which assure me of your
love and happiness, are sources to me of pure and boundless
joy.''[5]

Less than a year later, on June 23, 1840, when Mary was only
seventeen, she married Chesnut, then twenty-five. Not much is
known of their life during the next twenty years. Chesnut practiced
law in Camden and for ten years, 1842-1852, served in the state
legislature. In 1845 he and Mary went to London in the hope that
the sea voyage would benefit her health (which had always been
poor), and for the same reason they visited Saratoga Springs in the
summer of 1848. Chesnut served in the state senate from 1854
until 1858, when he entered the United States Senate as a state's
rights Democrat. He was a strong supporter of the Southern position and on November 10, 1860, shortly after Lincoln's election,
he resigned his seat in the Senate and returned to South Carolina to
help lead the fight for secession. The two years in Washington
were a happy time for Mary. She and her husband made many

friends among the capital's elite, and she greatly enjoyed the social and intellectual stimulus of their associations.

In February 1861, Mary went to Montgomery, where her husband, as a member of the Provisional Congress, helped organize the Southern Confederacy and elect Jefferson Davis President. During the break between the first and second sessions she went to Charleston and there, on April 12, 1861, she witnessed the attack on Fort Sumter. "At half past four," she wrote, "I sprang out of bed and on my knees, prostrate I prayed as I never prayed before."* But when the fort surrendered, without loss of life, after thirty-six hours of bombardment, she entered wholeheartedly into the joyful celebration. Late in April she went back to Montgomery for the second session of Congress and in June she joined her husband in Richmond, the new Confederate capital. Chesnut doubled as an aide to General Pierre Beauregard and as a member of Congress. His wife returned to South Carolina in September 1861, where she lived with her husband's parents at Mulberry until January 1862. She then moved to Columbia where her husband served for nine months on the South Carolina Executive Council. In October 1862, Davis called Chesnut back to Richmond to serve as a presidential aide with the rank of colonel. Except for a six-month sojourn in Camden, May-October 1863, broken by a trip to her mother's home in Alabama in June, Mary lived in Richmond from October 1862 until May 1864. During this period Chesnut was away from home occasionally on missions for Davis. In May 1864, following Chesnut's appointment as commander of Confederate reserves in South Carolina, with rank of brigadier

---

*This quotation is from Mrs. Chesnut's postwar version. In the original account, written shortly after the attack on Fort Sumter, she stated: "The live long night I tossed about—at half past four we hear the booming of the cannon—I start up—dress & rush to my sisters in misery—we go on the housetop & see the shells bursting—They say our men are wasting ammunition."

general, Mary returned to her native state. She and her husband
lived most of the time in Columbia until February 1865, when
the approach of Sherman's forces required Chesnut to lead his
troops and drove Mary into exile, first to Lincolnton, North
Carolina, and then to Chester, South Carolina. In May 1865 she
and her husband returned to Camden. They resided temporarily at
Bloomsbury, one of the several plantation homes owned by the
senior James Chesnut. None of these places was destroyed during
the war. Mulberry was pillaged and damaged by Federal raiders
commanded by General Edward E. Potter, but it was restored and
is still standing. Mrs. Chesnut continued her diary until August
1865 but the entries became sparse and irregular, and their import
is one of utter depression. On May 16, 1865, she wrote: "We are
scattered, stunned, the remnant of heart left alive with us filled
with brotherly hate. We sit and wait until the drunken tailor who
rules the United States of America issues a proclamation and
defines our anomalous position." In mid-June she noted: "We are
shut in here, turned with our faces to a dead wall." The entry for
July 26, the last of her journal, save for a brief notation dated
August 2, written on a card and pinned to a page of the notebook,
began: "I do not write often now—not for want of something to
say—but from a loathing of all I see and hear—why dwell upon
it?"

Mary Chesnut spent about three of the four and one-half years
covered by her diary in Montgomery, Richmond, and Columbia.
City life gave her an opportunity to display one of her most
distinctive traits, that of gregariousness. At the end of a crowded
day in Charleston in March 1861, she wrote: "Last night as I
turned down the gas I said to myself: 'certainly this has been one of
the pleasantest days of my life' . . . so many pleasant people, so
much good talk; for after all it was talk, talk, talk!" Partly because
of dislike of her nonagenarian father-in-law (whom she described
as a "tyrant"), but mainly because of isolation, she abhorred
living at Mulberry or any of the other Chesnut plantations. On

August 31, 1861, she wrote: "We go home Monday, if I am able to travel. Already I feel the dread stillness and torpor of our Sahara at Sandy Hill creeping into my veins. It chills the marrow of my bones . . . I am revelling in the noise of city life." At Mulberry a few weeks later she noted: "There is nothing but frizzle-frazzle talked in this house . . . I would sleep on bare boards if I could once more be amidst the stir and excitement of a live world. These people have grown accustomed to dullness . . . I feel abandoned of God and man here in this dismal swamp." In 1863, after escape from a long stay in the country, she wrote: "I was daft with delight to get away from home."

Largely because of the exceptional opportunity it afforded for mingling with interesting people, Richmond was Mary's favorite abode. On June 10, 1861, she confided to her journal: "I am always ill. The name of my disease is longing to get away from here and go to Richmond." During the sixteen months in Richmond, despite cramped quarters and other deprivations, she enjoyed relatively good health; this suggests that the headache, indigestion, malaise, and debility that bedeviled her on the plantation before, during, and after the war, may have been psychosomatic.

In Richmond, Mary was a favorite among the city's most prominent families, including the Randolphs, the Stanards, and the Haxalls, as well as among the political and military leaders, such as the Davises, the Lees, the Prestons, the Hamptons, the Clays, and the Wigfalls. Mary's admission to the social uppercrust was due in part to her husband's wealth, political prominence, and closeness to Jefferson Davis. But her continuing popularity was attributable mainly to her own exceptional attractiveness as a person. Though not a beauty, she was good looking and always dressed to emphasize her best features. She had a delightful sense of humor and a warm outgoing personality. She talked easily and well, her prowess as a conversationalist being in no small part the result of her rich knowledge of history and literature. Throughout

Mary Boykin Chesnut

Mary Boykin Chesnut From a Portrait in Oil

(From Isabella D. Martin and Myrta Lockett Avary, eds., A Diary from Dixie As Written by Mary Boykin Chesnut, New York, D. Appleton & Company, 1905.)

her life she was an avid reader both of ancient and current writings. Her diary includes appreciative and knowledgeable references to Shakespeare, Milton, Dickens, Thackeray, Hugo, and Schiller. She was shocked by *Fanny* but stated that the book was "not nastier or coarser" than *Uncle Tom's Cabin* which she read more than once. Some French works she read in the original, including Dumas' *Maitre d'Armes*. John R. Thompson, editor of the *Southern Literary Messenger*, endeared himself to her by providing recently published books and current issues of *Blackwood's, Cornhill*, and other magazines. L.Q.C. Lamar of Mississippi, one of the most cultured of Richmond's younger set, occasionally came bearing books, and sometimes he lingered to converse pleasantly about literary gems familiar to both him and his charming hostess.

Men were strongly attracted to Mary Chesnut and she enjoyed their attention. After General Lee bowed low and gave her a warm smile at church in 1863, she noted in her diary: "I was ashamed of being so pleased. I blushed like a school girl." On April 27, 1861, in Montgomery, she recorded: "The President came across the aisle to speak to me at church today. He was very cordial and I appreciated the honour."* Two months later she noted that at a small gathering in Richmond "the President took a seat by me on the sofa where I sat . . . [and] talked for nearly an hour."** In January 1864, at a big party given by Senator Thomas J. Semmes of Louisiana, Mrs. Chesnut was talking to Senator Benjamin Hill of Georgia, as they stood between Richmond's social queens, Mrs. John Stanard and Mrs. George Randolph. President Davis startled and flattered her by offering her his arm and taking her for a long stroll up and down the large reception hall, telling her of his difficulties in administering the hard-pressed Confederacy. The climax of her friendship with Davis came during his brief visit to

---

*This quotation is from the postwar revision; not in the wartime original.
**From the postwar revision; not in the wartime original.

Columbia in October 1864, when he spent a few hours in the Chesnut residence. "I went out to the gate to meet the President," she wrote in her journal; "[he] met me most cordially, kissed me in fact." After breakfast, the two of them talked on the porch while her husband and the presidential aides toured the city. Later, Davis made a public address from her piazza, after which she served him a mint julep to refresh him for continuation of his travels.

Mary was always a bit awed by the President, but with his wife, Varina, her relations were, except for a brief clash in 1861, close and uninhibited. Their friendship dated back to prewar days in Washington when their husbands were colleagues in the Senate. They were drawn together by their similarity of background, interests, and personality. They were of about the same age, and both were intelligent, well-educated, well-read, socially accomplished, and sparkling in conversation. Their husbands were much alike in that they were reserved, dignified, proud, and somewhat unbending in attitude and demeanor. On March 2, 1861, twelve days after Davis's inauguration as Confederate President at Montgomery, Mary Chesnut wrote in her diary: "Mrs. Robert Smith . . . carried me to Mrs. Jeff Davis' room where she met me with open arms. What a chat—that was *two* hours. She told me all [the] Washington news." Two months later she noted: "Dined at President Davis'. taken to dinner by the Pres. had a jolly time. Mrs. Davis so witty." Following another lunch with the Confederacy's First Lady on May 20, 1861, Mrs. Chesnut observed: "Two days in my life have never passed so rapidly & pleasantly—every body *well* bred—no body disagreeable—no body unkind—all clever —some remarkably so."*

In Richmond, to which the Confederate government moved in June 1861, an estrangement developed between Mrs. Chesnut and Mrs. Davis. The rift was of short duration, and Mrs. Chesnut in the final version of her diary—the one used by Ben Ames Wil-

---

*All the quotations in this paragraph are from the original, wartime diary.

liams—removed all references to it. Her reason for doing so probably was that she intended to publish the diary and she did not want to offend Mrs. Davis. On June 15, 1883, she wrote Varina: "How I wish you could read over my Journal. I have been two years over looking it—copying—leaving my self out. You must see it before it goes to print, but that may not be just now . . . for I must over haul it again and again."[6] Obviously, Mrs. Chesnut would not have wanted Mrs. Davis to see the following comments that appear in the original version of the diary: June 27, 1861: "We dined with the President. Mrs. Davis & himself are coarse [Mrs. Chesnut, or someone else, tried to erase this word but it is still decipherable.] talking people." June 28, 1861: "Yesterday for fear of giving offence had to take tea for a second time with Mrs. Davis. She was not civil enough. Kept me bandied [?] about for a seat." June 29, 1861: "I continue to dine at Mrs. Davis' table but it not pleasant." [In her revision, the one used by Williams, Mrs. Chesnut wrote in the entry for June 29, 1861, the flatly contradictory statement: "It is pleasant at the President's table."] ". . . . Lamar . . . was desperately ill again last night. I think it provokes Mrs. Davis that such men praise me so. What a place this is now, every one hates each other. . . . Mrs. Davis & Jeff Davis prove themselves anything but well-bred by their talk." July 4, 1861: "Mrs. Davis was rude to me & I got Mrs. Preston to ask her what she meant. Ample apology made. . . . I carried some of the candy to Mr. Lamar. . . . [He] says the reason Mrs. Davis don't like me [is] that I take up with the Wigfalls. . . . The President was excessively complimentary. Mrs. D. and I had a touching reconciliation."

The reason for the rift between Mrs. Chesnut and Mrs. Davis was almost certainly that given by L.Q.C. Lamar. In June and July 1861, the Wigfalls and the Chesnuts were intimate friends. At this time the Davises and the Wigfalls, who had been cordial, were in the process of falling out. Louis T. Wigfall, a member of the Texas delegation in the Confederate Congress, was also serving as aide to the President and as commander of a battalion of Texas troops. When Davis on July 19 left for Manassas without informing Wigfall of his departure, the Texan was miffed; he was also disappointed that he and his command had no part in the first big battle of the war. After the battle Wigfall joined in criticism of Davis's long-time friend, Colonel Lucius B. Northrup, the Confederacy's commissary general, for the shortage of supplies which allegedly prevented Joseph E. Johnston's army from following up the victory at First Manassas. Furthermore, Wigfall had a weakness for liquor, and Davis may have believed a report making the rounds in Richmond that the Texan was on a drunk shortly after the fight at Manassas. Yet another blow to their relationship occurred after tension developed between Joseph E. Johnston and the President concerning Johnston's rank, and Wigfall sided with Johnston. The Chesnuts, especially Mary, were caught in the crossfire of the opposing groups. On July 18, Mary wrote in her diary: "Mrs. Wigfall came in & lodged her complaint against the Davis[es]. I said nothing. . . . In the evening Mrs. Davis sat with me ever so long—abused Mrs. Wigfall."

After the battle of First Manassas, while the breach between the Davises and the Wigfalls widened, the Chesnuts and the Davises were together more and more. As Mary's relationship with Varina became warmer, Mary cooled toward the Wigfalls. There was no open break, but when faced with the necessity of choosing between friendship with Varina and friendship with Charlotte Wigfall, Mary chose the former.

Mary's choice was a natural one because of their shared interests and similar personalities. They also tended to have similar views toward other people. While some of the Virginia bluebloods condescendingly referred to Mrs. Davis as a coarse Western woman, the President's wife regarded some of Richmond's reigning ladies as ponderous and dull, a view which the vivacious Mary Chesnut shared. In their get-togethers the two outlanders enjoyed laughing at the excessive solemnity of the FFVs. A powerful influence in deepening their friendship was the unflinching loyalty of the Chesnuts to the Davises during the bitter attack on the administration which began with the Confederacy's military reverses of early 1862 and continued throughout the war. In March 1865, while Mary was in refuge in Lincolnton, North Carolina, she recorded a surprise visit from her husband during which he said of President Davis: "Sometimes I think I am the only friend he has in the world. At these dinners which they give us everywhere I spoil sport, for I will not sit there and hear Jeff Davis abused. . . . I lost my temper. I told them . . . that Jeff Davis was a gentleman and a patriot with more brains than the assembled company. . . . In Washington when we left it, Jeff Davis ranked second to none—in intellect —maybe first from the south. . . . Now, they rave that he is nobody and never was. And she? Oh, you would think to hear them that he found her yesterday in a Mississippi swamp." In view of such staunch fidelity it is little wonder that Mrs. Davis went to Mary Chesnut's residence at Chester, South Carolina, as she fled southward after the fall of Richmond, for one final visit with her trusted friend. "[Some] people sent me things for Mrs. Davis," Mary wrote shortly afterward, "but, shame on them, there were [other] people here so base as to be afraid to befriend Mrs. Davis, thinking when the Yankees came, they would take vengeance on them for it."

Mrs. Chesnut chided the FFVs and the low country aristocrats of her own state for their snobbery. To one of the latter who remarked, "The Up Country are new people, it seems. The old blood of the cavalier [stays] near the salt water," she tartly replied: "We are new, fresh, handsome, full grown, wealthy, accomplished, agreeable, brave as the bravest." Yet, Mary herself was by no means devoid of hauteur. In her diary she repeatedly disparaged the poor whites or "sandhill tackeys" of her neighborhood. One group who came to the Chesnut plantation with their families seeking employment as overseers she described as "stupid, slow, heavy-headed louts." However, as she moved about the country during the war and had increased contact with the yeomanry, she seemed to become more tolerant of them. After being stranded all night with some lower class people in a small railway station near Weldon, North Carolina, when her train broke down, in late 1863, she wrote: "We talked easily . . . as if we had known each other all our lives . . . No questions were asked, no names given . . . and yet if these men and women were not gentry and of the best sort I do not know ladies and gentlemen when I see them."

The original version of Mary Chesnut's diary indicates that she had a touch of vanity. On March 16, 1861, she wrote: "I can make anybody love me if I choose." Someone—probably the diarist herself—tried to erase this sentence, but it can still be deciphered, with the aid of an ultraviolet light. On August 27, 1861, she wrote: "My old frantic lover, Gen. Fair [called]—he has been Consul at Brussels. . . . I remember when he made such desperate love to me I thought him hideous—now he is handsome & imposing."*

Despite the sophistication that she acquired from travel, reading, and varied associations, Mrs. Chesnut remained something of a prude. On February 25, 1861, at Montgomery, she complained that William H. Trescot was too "Frenchy" in some of the jokes he told her. Two days later whe wrote: "Sat with a Mr. Robert Smith. . . . He . . . told me he was a little tight when something happened. I always feel as if a man had no moral sense of right or wrong, or even decency, when he alludes to his own *intoxication*."** Yet, she was broadminded enough to record in her diary a humorous incident at a Richmond dinner party, as reported to her by her young nephew, John Chesnut, a captain of cavalry. Concerning one of the lady guests, Johnny wrote: "Her dress was none too high in the neck, and by no means tight fitting around her lovely, high-born FF[V] bosom. The oysters were red

---

*Neither of the quotations in this paragraph appears in the postwar revision of the diary.
**From the original, wartime version.

hot. One fell! She screamed! B———dived for it with a fork, fished it up in a thrice [trice]. . . . With a fork! Imagine! The muff. I should certainly have risked burning my fingers that time!''

Mary Chesnut's perceptiveness, her astuteness at appraising human nature, and her opportunity to observe at close range many of the South's influential personalities make her diary one of the most valuable commentaries on Confederate leadership. She was overly generous in her estimate of some, including Jefferson Davis, and she was too harsh in her judgment of others. But most of her comments had a high degree of validity, and many of them were phrased with a pungency that was as delightful as it was revealing. Of General Lee, whom she admired, she wrote early in the war: "Can anyone say they know . . . [him]? I doubt it! He looks so cold, quiet and grand.''* When she heard that James M. Mason was to represent the Confederacy in England, she stated: "My wildest imagination will not picture Mr. Mason as a diplomat. He will say 'chaw' for 'chew', and he will call himself 'Jeems', and he will wear a dress coat to breakfast. Over here, whatever a Mason does . . . is above law.''** Writing of Joseph E. Johnston on December 22, 1861, she quoted Hamilton Boykin's account of a hunting trip that he, Wade Hampton, and others made with the general before the war: "[Johnston] was a capital shot, better maybe than Wade & I but the bird was too high or too low, the dogs too far or too near. Things never exactly suited him and he did not get a shot. He was too hard to please, too fussy. Wade & I came home with a heavy bag. We . . . shot right and left, happy go lucky. . . . Joe Johnston would not risk his reputation as a capitol shot & got nothing. . . . He is brave as Caesar, or the most accomplished soldier, &c, &c, [but] he is never going to fight a battle. You'll see.'' On July 25, 1864, after listening to a South Carolinian's praise of Johnston, she wrote: "A general who is

*From postwar revision; not in the original version.
**From postwar revision; not in the original version.

known to disdain obedience to any order, who refuses to give the President any information for fear the President will betray him to the enemy—if that is not the madness of self-conceit, what is it?'' In Lincolnton, North Carolina, on February 22, 1865, she reported: "General Joseph E. Johnston joined us [for a walk]. He explained to us all of Lee's and Stonewall Jackson's mistakes. He was radiant and joyful. . . . He always impresses me with the feeling that all his sympathies are on the other side.''

In October 1863, Mary wrote: "Beauregard sulking in Charleston . . . He never had much brains . . . and now he is losing heart . . . Bragg, thanks to Longstreet and Hood . . . won Chickamauga; so we looked [for] results that would pay for our losses in battle, at least. Certainly they would capture Rosencrantz. [But] no! There sits Bragg [like] a good dog, howling on his hind legs before Chattanooga. . . . He always stops to quarrel with his generals.'' The diary entry for March 15, 1864, states: "General Hampton came with his troubles. Stuart had taken one of Hampton's Brigades and given it to Fitzhugh Lee. General H[ampton] complained of this to General Lee who told him curtly: 'I would not care if you went back to South Carolina with your whole division.' Wade said his manner made this speech immensely mortifying. . . . It seems General Lee has no patience with any personal complaints or grievances. He is all for the cause.''

Mary devoted more space in her diary to John Bell Hood than to any other general. Her comments had to do mainly with Hood's courtship of Sally Buchanan "Buck" Preston, daughter of Mary's most intimate friends, General and Mrs. John S. Preston of Columbia, South Carolina. The twice-wounded Hood went to Richmond in November 1863, to recuperate from the loss of his right leg at Chickamauga. In his wartime photographs the thirty-two-year-old general, peering solemnly over a formidable array of whiskers, looks anything but the gay Lothario, but Richmond gossip in December 1863, had him engaged at one and the same time to four of the capital's reigning belles, one of whom, the lovely Louise Wigfall, many years later recalled him as ''a man of singular simplicity of character and charm of manner—boyish in his enthusiasm—superbly handsome, with beautiful blue eyes, golden hair . . . broadshouldered, tall and erect—a noble man of undaunted courage and blameless life.'' During his three months in Richmond in the winter of 1863-1864, Hood hobbled about on his crutches to receive adulation and acclaim at a dizzying round of parties, charades, and dances. Of all the attractive people whom he met, the one who dazzled him most was ''Buck'' Preston. Mrs. Chesnut, a woman not given to extravagance, especially when portraying other members of her sex, described her as ''the very sweetest woman I ever knew . . . the darling . . . I would not have if I could anything altered about her mentally, morally, physically.'' Hood, largely under Mary Chesnut's discerning eye, pursued the lovely young woman with the same impetuosity and aggressiveness that he displayed in attacking Yankees on the field of battle. As Mrs. Chesnut records the romance, ''Buck'' was flattered by the attentions of the military hero, and for a while she responded to his amorous designs even to the extent of becoming engaged. But she was repelled by his naiveté, his maladroitness, and his importunity. After Hood left the capital, her interest turned to other suitors.

Mrs. Chesnut's own initial admiration of Hood cooled considerably during his sojourn in Richmond. She became convinced that the general was trying to use his associations with Davis and the President's intimates to promote his military fortunes. On January 1, 1864, she told Hood: ''You are an awkward flatterer. You ought to praise me to somebody who will tell J[ames] C[hesnut]—and vice versa. Man and wife are too made one to receive a compliment shared [?] in the face [?] that way with grace.'' In her entry of February 13, 1864, she quotes Hood as saying to her: ''The President was finding fault with some of his officers in command and I said: 'Mr. President, why don't you come and lead us yourself? I would follow you to the death.' ''

Mary responded perceptively and bluntly: "If you stay here in Richmond much longer you will grow to be a courtier! You came a rough Texan!"

Some of Mrs. Chesnut's most caustic remarks were about politicians. On April 3, 1861, in Charleston, she wrote: "Met the lovely Lucy Holcombe, now Mrs. Governor Pickens. . . . Old Pick was there with a better wig."* A year later she referred to Pickens as "the Great Buzzfuzzy." On February 20, 1864, she reported: "At Mrs. Davis's met . . . Senator Clay. Heavens! He knows how to quarrel!" She was especially critical about the stormy and erratic senator from Texas, Louis T. Wigfall, whose ability she recognized and appreciated, but whose excesses in drink, in speech, and hatred she greatly deplored. On December 29, 1864, at Columbia, she noted in her diary: "Wigfall is here. [He says] 'Make Joe Johnston dictator and all will be well . . . Hood is dead, smashed, gone up forever.' . . . Wigfall himself, from whom we hoped so much . . . has only been . . . destructive."

The principal fault that Mary found with Confederate leaders was their quarrelsomeness—their inability to work together for the common good. On March 9, 1861, at Montgomery, while her husband was helping launch the Southern government, she observed: "We are abusing one another as fiercely as ever we abused the Yankees." On June 19, 1861, she wrote: "Every man wants to be at the head of affairs himself." Six weeks later, she denounced Beauregard's criticism of Jefferson Davis for failure to follow up the victory won at First Manassas as a manifestation of incredible "conceit and self-assertion." On October 3, 1861, she stated: "If the Confederacy had chosen to elect Barnwell Rhett President . . .

---

*The first sentence of this quotation is from the postwar revision; the second is from the wartime original. Williams, p. 32, quotes the two sentences as if they were from the same source, thus: "Met the lovely Lucy Holcombe, now Mrs. Governor Pickens last night at the Isaac Hayness. Old Pick has a better wig."

or had Mr. Davis made Barnwell Rhett Secretary of State, we
might have escaped one small war at least; the war the [Charleston]
Mercury [is] . . . waging with the Administration." Mrs. Chesnut
early recognized dissension, nurtured by ambition, pride, and
excessive individualism, as one of the South's greatest handicaps.
On August 29, 1861, she expressed concern about the impotence
of an "armed democracy" whose "chiefs quarrel among themselves." A month later she denounced "the senseless abuse
heaped on Jeff Davis" and added: "Republics, everybody jawing,
everybody putting their mouths in, nothing sacred, all confusion of
babble, crimination, and recrimination—republics can't carry on a
war." She might well have added that republics founded on the
principle of state's rights and dominated by planters, each of
whom was accustomed to the role of petty sovereign, proud,
provincial, and resentful of criticism, could not carry on wars.
Certainly she was aware of these qualities, for she observed and
condemned them in James Chesnut, Sr., her father-in-law. On
October 19, 1862, she complained that faction was "the rock on
which we split." In October 1863, in reporting the hassle between
Bragg and his generals at Chattanooga, and the proposal to restore
Joseph E. Johnston to command in the West, she wrote: "The
President detests Joe Johnston for all the trouble he has given him
and Gen[era]l Joe returns the compliment with compound interest.
His hatred of Jeff Davis amounts to a religion." A year later, as she
saw the mantle of defeat settling over the Confederacy, she observed: "We crippled ourselves—blew ourselves up—by intestine
strife."

Mrs. Chesnut manifested almost as much concern with Negroes
and slavery as with Confederate leadership. Her attitude toward
the South's "peculiar institution" was characterized by ambival-
ence. As did many other enlightened Southerners of her time, she
regarded slavery as a great evil. What she loathed most about the
system was its corrupting influence on the white men of the South.
On March 18, 1861, at Montgomery she wrote: "God for-

give us, but ours is a *monstrous* system, & wrong, & iniquity.
. . . Like the patriarchs of old, our men live all in one house with
their wives & their concubines; & the mulattoes one sees in every
family partly resemble the white children & every lady tells you
who is the father of all the mulatto children in everybody's household but those in her own, she seems to think drop from the clouds.
. . . My disgust sometimes is boiling over.''* She hated slavery but
she thoroughly enjoyed the conveniences and comforts that it
afforded, such as breakfast in bed, anticipation and prompt filling
of all her needs by a personal attendant wherever she went,
complete relief from household chores, and the satisfaction of
having a faithful companion who would share all her woes, agree
emphatically with whatever she said, and shower her with compliments when her ego needed replenishment. ''I hate slavery,''**
she wrote in her diary on November 27, 1861, but in the same
entry, and in several others as well, she denounced as self-
righteous and hypocritical those Northerners, especially Harriet
Beecher Stowe, who condemned the institution. She argued that
slaves were more of a care than a blessing and that the only persons
who benefited substantially from slavery were the Negroes themselves and the Yankees who grew rich from business generated by
slave labor. While staying with her father-in-law at Mulberry in
June 1861, she wrote: ''There are sixty or seventy people kept here
to wait upon this household, two-thirds of them too old or too
young to be of any use. But families remain intact.''*** Six
months later she observed: ''I doubt if ten thousand in money ever
comes to this old gentleman's hands. . . . [His money] goes to
support a horde of idle, dirty Africans, while he is abused and

*From the original wartime version; not in postwar revision.
**From the postwar revision; whether this phrase appeared in the war-
time version cannot be ascertained, because, as previously noted, the
only portions of Mrs. Chesnut's diary identifiable as ''original'' extend
only through October 1, 1861.
***From the postwar revision; not in the original version.

vilified [by Northerners] as a cruel slave owner. I say we are no
better than our judges in the North and no worse.'' The frequency
and zeal with which Mary denounced critics of slavery bear out
Queen Gertrude's observation in Hamlet that ''the lady doth protest too much,'' and evidence a deepseated feeling of guilt that
made Southerners hypersensitive and contentious, helped bring on
their secession, and greatly impeded their bid for independence.[7]

Of Negroes in general, Mary had a very low opinion. In March
1862, she wrote: ''The best way to take Negroes to your heart is to
get as far away from them as possible. . . . People can't love things
dirty, ugly, repulsive simply because they ought.'' More than once
she referred to the blacks as animals; in August 1864, she wrote:
''It takes but one moment for these creatures to go back to their
naked savage, animal nature.'' She found evidence of Negro
savagery in several instances of slaves murdering their owners.
One case involved the smothering of her aged, widowed cousin,
Betsy Witherspoon, who was killed as she lay in her bed, by her
pampered house servants. On hearing of the murder, Mrs. Chesnut
observed on September 21, 1861: ''Hitherto I have never thought
of being afraid of Negroes. I had never injured any of them; why
should they want to hurt me? . . . Somehow today I feel that the
ground is cut away from under my feet.''

Mrs. Chesnut commented repeatedly on what she regarded as
the Negroes' opportunism and duplicity. She cited an instance
involving a group of South Carolina slaves, whose owner had fled
on the approach of the Federals. When the Yankees moved on, the
owner returned to his plantation with a group of Confederate
soldiers. The Negroes greeted him with a show of great rejoicing.
After being secretly warned by one of the blacks not to trust the
ostensibly loyal Negroes, the owner disguised himself as a Federal
officer and that night visited the slave quarters. He was greeted
with the statement: ''Massa you come for ketch rebels? We show

you whey you can ketch thirty tonight.'' They then led him to the Confederate camp where presumably they were apprehended by those whom they sought to betray.

Mrs. Chesnut did not hold all Negroes in low esteem. A few whom she came to know well she treated as full-fledged human beings and attributed to them qualities more admirable than were shown by some of the whites. Some of the most interesting and revealing entries in her diary told of conversations that she had with her colored attendants. When Sherman's troops passed through South Carolina in 1865, the Chesnut Negroes, with only one exception, remained faithful to their masters and the conduct of some transcended passive loyalty. One slave, Isaac McLaughlin, returned intact a box of silver that Mary Chesnut entrusted to him for safekeeping during the invasion. Ellen, a maid, to whom she committed her diamonds, kept them throughout the emergency, and then, in Mary's words, ''handed them back to me with as little apparent interest in the matter as if they were garden peas.'' Of another faithful servant she wrote: ''The plantation and mills—Mulberry House &c &c [were] saved by Claiborne, that black rascal [who was] suspected by all the world! Claiborne boldly affirmed that Mr. Chesnut would not be hurt by destroying his place. They would only hurt Negroes, [that] Mars' Jeems hardly ever came there and only took a little something . . . to eat when he came.''

Slavery was only one of several aspects of Southern society and mores on which *A Diary from Dixie* threw valuable light. Mrs. Chesnut reported numerous manifestations of class consciousness and caste. In her entry of March 18, 1861, for example, she told of a Confederate congressman complaining of having to associate with the riffraff on a train ride from Montgomery to Charleston. ''Mr. ——— will not please the democracy,'' she wrote, ''he said aloud in the cars he wished we had separate coaches like the English & get away from those whiskey drinking, tobacco chewing rascals &c—rabble.''* Mary added her own comment about her traveling companions: ''Each supposed he was one of the gentlemen to be separated from the other thing.'' As previously noted, Mary resented the exclusiveness of the FFVs, but it was the ostentatious display of aristocratic pretensions that annoyed her rather than class distinction. On March 12, 1864, she quoted approvingly Sally Preston's comment on a Virginian's complaint that a low-born person had infiltrated the capital's high society: ''Until we came here we never heard of our social position. . . . To talk of that sort of thing seems so vulgar. Down our way that sort of thing was settled beyond a peradventure . . . like the earth and the sky. We never gave it a thought.'' Mrs. Chesnut readily admitted that some of the South's aristocracy were less than courtly in their demeanor. As an example, she cited Mrs. William H. Trescot, wife of President James Buchanan's assistant secretary of war, who, according to the English journalist William H. Russell, vulgarly stood on her back porch and ''screamed for the Negroes three fields off.''** But Mary Chesnut regarded such ladies as exceptional. ''Our women,'' she wrote, ''are soft and sweet, low-toned, indolent, graceful, quiescent.'' She was certain that the real gentry were a superior group. In support of her conviction, she quoted a hospital matron's testimony that among sick and wounded soldiers ''those born in the purple, the gentry, those who are accustomed to a life of luxury . . . are better patients. They endure in silence. They are hardier, stronger, tougher, less liable to break down than sons of the soil. Why? . . . [because of] the something in man that is more than the body.''

Mrs. Chesnut was fully aware that the courtliness she observed among her fellow Southerners was accompanied by fierce pride and a propensity to violence. On August 3, 1861, in reporting an altercation between some aristocratic South Carolinians and

*From the original, wartime version.
**From the original, wartime version, entry of May 9, 1861.

Marylanders over competing claims to a camp site, she wrote: "These foolish, rash, hair-brained Southern lads . . . are thrilling with fiery ardor. The red-hot Southern martial spirit is in the air. These young men, however, were all educated abroad, and it is French or German ideas that they are filled with. . . . These quarrelsome young soldiers have lovely manners . . . [and] are so sweet tempered."* In recording a conversation with some friends in Columbia, South Carolina, on June 12, 1862, she attributed to one of them the comment: "Men may be dishonest, immoral, cruel, black with every crime. [But] take care of how you say so unless you are a crack shot and willing to risk your life in defense of your words. For as soon as one defamatory word is spoken, pistols come at once to the fore. That is South Carolina ethics. . . . If you have stout hearts—and good family connections—you can do pretty much as you please."

With all their shortcomings, Mary Chesnut still rated Southerners as distinctly superior to Northerners, whom she often represented as pushy, power-hungry, materialistic, self-righteous, and hypocritical. But she apparently conceded some validity to General Winfield Scott's observation early in the war that if the contest could be decided by one wild desperate dash, the Southerners would win. They could bear pain without a murmur, but they lacked the Northerners' patience, their willingness to submit to discipline, and their capacity to endure. After paraphrasing Scott's comparison, Mary made the comment: "A nice prospect for us."

Mary Chesnut realized the importance of the clan concept and the idea of personal leadership in shaping Southern society and in fighting the war initiated at Sumter. In a discerning and delightful characterization of her nephew, Captain Johnny Chesnut, a

*From the revised version: The original states: "Ransom Calhoun & Willie Preston have come and nearly had a fight for the ground with a Maryland Regiment to picket their horses. Oh my countrymen, why will you be so overbearing & quarrelsome!"

twenty-three-year-old South Carolina aristocrat who had large
holdings of land and slaves, she wrote:

> He does not care for books . . . [though] he took his diploma at
> the South Carolina College. . . . He knows nothing of politics
> and cares less. . . . He rides like an Arab and loves his horses
> in the same way. . . . I think he is happiest when he sends one
> of his fine horses to some girl who is worthy to ride such a
> horse. She must be beautiful and graceful. Then, superbly
> mounted, he goes to ride with her. He is sure to go slowly
> along where everybody can see them, and can admire the
> horses and the girl. Strange to say he has not one jot of
> personal vanity. . . . I do not think he has an idea what we are
> fighting about, and he does not want to know. He says "My
> company—my men"—with a pride, a faith and an affection
> which is sublime.

Mrs. Chesnut loved the compliments heaped on her by admiring
Southern gentlemen, though she frankly characterized some of
their effusions as "blarney," and she was too smart not to realize
that Southern gentility was sometimes much less genuine than it
seemed. She reported overhearing a group of South Carolina
aristocrats saying of one of their associates: "What a perfect
gentleman! So fine looking, high-bred, distinguished, easy, free
and above all graceful in his bearing. So high-toned! He is always
indignant at any symptom of wrong-doing. . . . [But] then the other
side of the picture is true too. You can always find him! You know
where to find him. Wherever there is a looking glass, a bottle or a
woman; there will he be also."* The diarist then noted: "[They

---

*Mrs. Chesnut first wrote the sentence: "Wherever there is a looking
glass, a bottle of whiskey or a Negro woman; there will he be also." But
she crossed out the words "of whiskey or a Negro" and inserted "or"
before "woman."

were discussing] a complicated character . . . [with] what Mrs.
Preston calls the refinement spread thin, skin deep only.''

Southern society as portrayed by Mrs. Chesnut was dominated
by males, a circumstance which she deeply resented. She quoted
Mrs. Mat Singleton's complaint to her and a group of friends:
''Men here are masters, and they find fault and bully you. You are
afraid of them, and take a meek, timid, defensive style.'' In hearty
agreement Mary chimed in: ''Dogmatic man rarely speaks at home
but to find fault. . . . At every word the infatuated fool of a woman
recoils as if she had received a slap in the face; and for dear life she
begins to excuse herself for what is no fault of hers. . . . She seems
to be expected to put right every wrong in the world.'' On February
16, 1864, she wrote: ''South Carolina as a rule does not think it
necessary for women to have any existence outside of their pan-
tries or nurseries. If they have none, let them nurse the bare walls.
But for men!, the pleasures of all the world are reserved.'' She
objected to man's masterful stance principally because of her
conviction that he was often less capable than the woman whom he
held in subordination. This she considered to be true in the case of
her parents-in-law. On November 30, 1861, she wrote: ''Old Mr.
Chesnut . . . sees his fine estates slipping away from him. These
are his Gods; he worships his own property. . . . Mrs. Chesnut with
all her angelic mildness, sweetness &c has a talent for organizing,
training, making things comfortable, and to move without noise
and smoothly. He roars and shouts if a pebble of an obstacle is put
in his way. Somehow, I find her the genius of the place.''

Perhaps *A Diary from Dixie* is most important for its candid and
intimate view of the relationship between the diarist and her
husband during a time critical for them, their class, and their
region. Although they were of similar background, they were
markedly different in personality and interests. In contrast to her
vivacity and volatility was his reserve and quiet dignity. She was
an omnivorous reader, but there is nothing in her diary to indicate

that he shared her interest in books. Mary sometimes became impatient with her husband because of his lack of aggressiveness. On April 27, 1861, she wrote: "Mr. Chesnut asleep to go at 7 o'clock with Wade Hampton to see Jeff Davis—Oh if I could put some of my reckless spirit into these discreet, cautious lazy men." Another source of friction was her occasional, though apparently rare, use of opium to relieve pain. On July 26, 1861, she noted: "Mrs. Davis [and] Wigfall . . . sat with me & told me unutterable stories of the war—but I forget after so much opium—Mr. Chesnut would not go to bed but sat up & gave me such a scolding."

Both of the Chesnuts occasionally were prone to jealousy. On a train ride from Camden to Charleston in March 1861, handsome ex-Governor John Manning came into the Chesnuts' coach and said that he was seeking a seat for a young lady traveling in his care. James Chesnut graciously yielded his place; a little later Manning returned and, according to Mary, "threw himself cheerfully down in the vacant place [and] cooly remarked 'I am the young lady.' " She added: "He is always the handsomest man alive." A few days later she had dinner with Manning and some others while her husband was visiting troops in a nearby camp. It was on the next day that she wrote that Chesnut angrily accused her of flirting with Manning. A few weeks later when another friend, William H. Trescot, came to the Richmond hotel where the Chesnuts were staying and inquired for James, Mary told him to wait on the stairs while she went up to get her husband. When she entered the room and told James her mission, he, in Mrs. Chesnut's words "locked the door and put the key in his pocket. [He] said I should not be running up and down stairs on Trescot's errands."* The next day Trescot angrily told her that he had waited on the steps for an hour.

But the shoe was sometimes on the other foot. One Sunday in

*From the original, wartime version, July 24, 1861; not in the postwar revision.

1863, when the Chesnuts turned a corner in Richmond on their walk to church, they suddenly encountered "a very handsome woman" who immediately rushed up to James, extended her hands and said: "So glad [to see you]—did not know you had come . . . When did you come? And you have not been to see me &c &c." Mary waited in vain for an introduction. As husband and wife resumed their walk, Mary inquired "who is it?" James replied: "Don't know. Never saw the woman before in my life. She evidently took me for somebody else." After relating the incident in her diary, Mary added: "The subject was renewed again and again, until it became a screaming farce, but he stuck to his formula. 'Never saw the woman before in my life—took me for somebody else'*. . . . 'What a credulous fool you must take me to be.' "

In May 1864, on a train trip Mary Chesnut accidentally became separated from her husband and was stranded for a few hours in Kingsville, South Carolina. When she went to a hotel, she was refused a room by the proprietress, whom she described as "a very haughty and highly painted dame." The woman did not at first recognize Mrs. Chesnut, although the two women had once been schoolmates in Charleston. After James rejoined her at Manchester, Mary informed him that the painted woman "told me she had not seen me for twenty years but that she met you constantly." His reply, according to Mary, was: "God bless my soul, I never saw the woman in my life."

Despite the fact that the Chesnuts were rich and that Mary had funds of her own, money was a source of friction in their marriage. James considered her extravagant in her expenditures for entertainment, clothing, and things of small importance. On January 8, 1864, Mary wrote: "I was to take Miss Cary to [a charade at] Mrs. Semmes. J. C. inquired the price of the carriage. [I replied] 25

*Here Williams inserted the words "My teasing retort"; but Mrs. Chesnut may very well not have been teasing.

dollars an hour. Then he cursed by all his Gods—such extravagance, such stupid charades. . . . Then [he] quieted down. . . . I did
not dream of asking him to go with me after that lively overture [till
he said]: 'I did intend to go with you, but you do not ask me.' [I
responded] . . . 'I have been asking you for twenty years to go with
me—in vain.' '' The angry husband went to the charade and when
the party returned home near daylight, Mary, as she wrote later,
"had the pleasure to see J. C. like a man stand and pay for that
carriage.''

The principal cause of tension between Mary and James was her
love of partying and his contrary attitude which ranged from
reluctant assent to vigorous opposition. During the winter of
1862-1863, when the South Carolina belles, "Buck" and Mary
Preston, spent a month with the Chesnuts in their Richmond
apartment, partying was practically continuous. Mrs. Chesnut
later wrote of this happy period: "We danced—to the music of an
old ramshackle piano—and had a good time generally. . . . At first
Mr. Chesnut was too civil by half. I knew it could not last, [his]
going everywhere with us, to parties, to concerts, to private
theatricals, [and] even to breakfasts. Then he broke down and
denounced us for being so dissipated. Mr. Davis came to our relief
and sent the recalcitrant head of our household to inspect and
report [on] Charleston and on Southern armies generally.'' The
following winter Mary, despite James' periodic protests, again
indulged her bent for socializing. The consequences she recorded
thus in a diary entry of December 10, 1863: "J. C. laid the law
down last night. I felt it to be the last drop in my full cup. [He said]
'No more feasting in this house! This, is no time for junketing and
merry-making. There is a positive want of proper feeling in the life
you lead.' '' She reminded him of his statement that he brought her
to Richmond to enjoy one more winter before returning to the
doldrums of South Carolina, but to no avail. As she put it, in
apparent resignation, "he is the master of the house. To hear is to
obey.'' But she was not as acquiescent as she claimed. Soon, on

one pretext or another—and once in connivance with Mrs. Davis—she reentered the social whirl. Sometimes James went along, and if the Richmond beauties such as Hetty Cary (whom Chesnut described as "fascinating") were especially attentive, he could be surprisingly amiable. But always his true nature would soon reassert itself and he would again lay down the law—"No more parties."

In his introduction to *A Diary from Dixie* Ben Ames Williams refers to the journal as a "heart-warming story of the deep, fine love between Mrs. Chesnut and her husband." Unquestionably the relationship was characterized by mutual respect, and there were times when it was truly harmonious. One such occasion she described thus in the diary entry of March 24, 1862: "The night I came from Mad[ame] Tognos instead of making a row about the lateness of the hour, he said he was 'so wide awake and so hungry.' So I put on my dressing gown, and scrambled some eggs, there on our own fire. And with our feet on the fender and the small supper table between us we enjoyed the supper and the glorious gossip. Rather a pleasant state of things, when one's own husband is in good humor and cleverer than all the men outside."

In a good marriage chatty, companionable, and leisurely evenings such as that described by Mary on this occasion would be frequent. But she makes so much of this instance, the only one of its sort recorded anywhere in her journal, as to leave the impression that it was unusual, if not unique.

There are many other passages in the diary that make difficult the acceptance of Williams' estimate of it as a "heart-warming story of . . . deep fine love." As early as March 11, 1861, Mary wrote: "Mr. C[hesnut] thinks himself an open, frank, confiding person and required an answer to this proposition. Truth required me to say that I knew no more of what Mr. C. thought or felt on any subject [now] than I did twenty years before. Sometimes I feel that we understand each other a little—ever so little—then up goes the iron wall between us. He never gives me the impression of an insincere person, or even a cold one, only reticent, like an Indian, his pride is to hide all feeling.''* On December 7, 1863, she told of weeping profusely at the sight of a woman in Richmond throwing herself in bitter lamentation on the coffin of her husband. She added: ''J. C. could see me and everything that he loved hung, drawn and quartered without moving a muscle.'' When Mary told him that he was as undemonstrative as an Indian, he answered "in unmoved tones": '' 'So could any civilized man! Savages, however—Indians at least—are more dignified in that particular than we are. Noisy fidgitty grief never moves me at all; it annoys me. Self-control you need. You think yourself a miracle of sensibility, [but] self-control is what you need. That is all that separates you from those you look down upon as unfeeling.' ''

In trying to evaluate the Chesnuts' marital relationship, consideration must be taken of the fact that Mary's diary is the account of only one member of the partnership, that it treats of a relatively brief period of their life together, and that this was a time during which war—and a losing war at that—created unusual stresses and disruptions. There is evidence in the diary that the marriage of these two dissimilar people was undergirded by genuine affection and that the misfortunes experienced near the end of the war fostered an understanding and an appreciation of each other unknown in their prior years together.

Little is known of Mrs. Chesnut's life during the period following termination of her diary in August 1865. She continued to live in Camden to which she and her husband had returned in May. During the first months of Reconstruction she suffered periods of depression but with the passing of time her morale improved. The poor health to which she had always been susceptible continued to plague her as long as she lived. In quest of health and relief from

*Whether this statement, dated March 11, 1861, and written on a loose, legal size leaf, was written during the war or afterward is uncertain.

Camden's summer heat, she and her husband made occasional trips to the spas of Virginia and New York.

The Chesnuts had no children to brighten the loneliness of their postwar years. Undoubtedly Mary's failure to become a mother was one of the greatest disappointments of her life. The diary entry for March 21, 1861, in the original version, contains the statement: "Me a childless wretch . . . God help me, no good have I done." A few months later she wrote: "Women need maternity to bring out their best and their true loveliness."* Much of the affection that she might have bestowed on the children denied to her she showered on the offspring of others, including the sons and daughters of her sister, Kate Williams.

In 1873 the Chesnuts moved into a stately new home, Sarsfield, a Norman villa-type of residence located in Camden and built of old brick hauled from Mulberry. Mary was said to have inspected the new home many times during its construction. James Chesnut died at Sarsfield in 1885.

Long before her husband's death, Mary had begun to revise and rewrite her diary. A notation dated 1875 in one of three original volumes indicates that she was rereading the diary at that time. This notation, inserted after a self-laudatory entry of March 1861, states: "Reading this Journal I find I was a vain and foolish old woman—to record silly flattery to myself—In short an old idiot." Mrs. Chesnut's letter of June 15, 1883, to Varina Davis shows that she had been engaged in revision for two years and that portions of the journal were rewritten more than once.

One of the last surviving papers of Mrs. Chesnut is her will, written in her own hand and dated January 28, 1886. In this document she bequeathed most of her estate to her nephew, sister Kate's son, David R. Williams, who lived with her at Sarsfield after James Chesnut's death. To David's brother, S. Miller Wil-

*From the postwar revision; not in the original version.

liams, she willed the furniture known as " the Gov. Miller furniture," which she had inherited from her father; and to her niece, Serena Chesnut Williams, she left "my diamond ring and my two Jersey cows, Olly and Flora."[8]

Mary Chesnut died on November 22, 1886. In accordance with a stipulation in her will she was buried by her husband's side in the Chesnut family cemetery at Knights Hill, Camden.

2

Virginia Tunstall Clay—
Alabama Belle

Virginia Clay-Clopton, reminiscing in her seventies after the death of her first and second husbands, Clement Clay and David Clopton, remarked:"I was an hereditary believer in States' Rights . . .; from my earliest girlhood three lessons had been taught me religiously, viz: to be proud alike of my name and blood and section; to read my Bible; and, last, to know my 'Richmond Enquirer.' "[1] This statement reveals far more of the character and personality of the person who made it than she probably realized; indeed, it provides the key to understanding her career.

Virginia Caroline Tunstall, born on January 16, 1825, in Nash County, North Carolina, was the only child of Dr. Peyton Randolph Tunstall and Ann (Arrington) Tunstall. Her own and her father's first names suggest that her paternal antecedents were Virginians but no documentary evidence has been found to support this conjecture. Virginia lost her twenty-year-old mother at the age of three and the widowed father took her to Alabama to be reared by his wife's relatives. She grew up in Tuscaloosa and its environs, living first in the home of an uncle, Henry Watkins Collier, who in 1837 became chief justice of the Alabama Supreme Court, and later residing with another uncle, Alfred Battle, a wealthy planter.

Both the Colliers and the Battles belonged to the community's gentry. Virginia, attended by slaves and surrounded by a plenitude of congenial cousins, entered heartily into a life abounding with play, partying, and dancing, though some of her Methodist relatives regarded dancing as a sin. She probably received her first academic training from plantation tutors. At the age of twelve she began two years of formal schooling at a Tuscaloosa institution presided over successively by an English woman and a native of New England. As in the case of Mrs. Jefferson Davis, some of her best education came from a male acquaintance who taught her because of a deep personal interest, inspired by her brightness and charm. Virginia's informal tutor was her father's bachelor brother, Thomas B. Tunstall, Alabama secretary of state. Many years later she wrote: "My memory crowds with pictures of my Uncle Tom, walking slowly up and down, playing his violin, and interspersing his numbers with some wise counsel to the child beside him. He taught me orally of poetry, and music, of letters and philosophy, and of the world's great interests. He early instilled in me a pride of family while reading to me [Sir Walter] Scott's fine tribute to Brian Tunstall." In the company of her father, who visited her occasionally, and of her Uncle Tom, she attended a theatrical performance in Mobile, "The Gamester," featuring Charles Kean and Ellen Tree. She wept so profusely over a death scene that some members of the audience focused their attention on her more than on the actors.[2]

In 1839, at fourteen years of age, Virginia entered the Nashville Female Academy, from which she received a diploma in December 1840. Little is known of her life in the Tennessee capital, but a return visit there in 1865 elicited from her the reminiscent statement: "It made me sad to drive thru Cherry, Summer, College & other streets, where more than twenty (!) years ago I promenaded with my college lovers, in all the unalloyed exuberance of pristine puppy love."[3] So, despite the academy's strict rules and the narrow conventions of the period, she apparently had a good time.

When she returned to Tuscaloosa about the time of her sixteenth birthday, she was one of the most popular members of a social set that contained an impressive number of charming young women. Many youthful aristocrats vied for her favor, but the successful suitor was Clement Claiborne Clay of Huntsville, Alabama, to whom she became engaged soon after her graduation from the Nashville Female Academy. Clay was perhaps the most sought after young bachelor in Tuscaloosa society. His father, Clement Comer Clay, a wealthy lawyer-planter of Huntsville and an alumnus of Blount College, predecessor of the University of Tennessee, had been congressman, governor of Alabama, United States senator, and in 1842 was a member of the Alabama Supreme Court. The senior Clay, a strong advocate of education, sent his three children, Clement Claiborne, John Withers, and Hugh Lawson, to the University of Virginia and all three of them became lawyers. Clement, the eldest, was the best educated of the three, earning an A. B. degree from the University of Alabama and a law degree from the University of Virginia. He was also the most successful. He was frail throughout his life because of chronic asthma and other afflictions. But lack of robustness did not deprive him of spunk. He once attacked some school bullies who abused his younger brothers and proudly reported the incident to his father.

When Clement Claiborne Clay began courting Virginia Tunstall, he had just become a member of the Alabama legislature. He revealed an awareness of his popularity in a humorous note to his brother, December 20, 1842: "I have been to numerous parties & am a sort of lion, because of *my honors, single-blessedness* & good looks & manners." In the same letter he revealed the precariousness of his single-blessedness with the comment: "There is a most lovely & beautiful young lady here who has quite *mesmerized* me."[4] Less than six weeks later, on February 1, 1843, this young lady became his bride. The wedding, held in the residence of Virginia's uncle, Henry W. Collier, was a grand affair, attended by members of the legislature, the president and faculty of the University of Alabama, and many other prominent people. During the courtship, Clement had asked his parents about the advisability of assuming new responsibilities amidst the persistent economic depression that had piled up the Clay family's debts. They apparently encouraged him to abandon his bachelorhood. Two days after the wedding, he wrote his father: "Virginia & I were married . . . at 7 o'clock. . . . Virginia was very much agitated, but I was far more composed than I had any idea I could be."[5]

When the legislature adjourned two weeks after the nuptials, the twenty-six-year-old groom took his eighteen-year-old bride to his parents' home in Huntsville. They made the long trip by stage coach over a road sometimes so rocky as to compel them to leave the carriage and proceed on foot. But the end, as recalled by Virginia after an interval of sixty years, was joyous:

> We arrived in Huntsville on the evening of the second day of our journey. Our driver . . . touched up the spirited horses as we crossed the Public Square and blew a bugle blast as we wheeled round the corner; when fairly dashing down Clinton Street, he pulled up in a masterly style in front of 'Clay Castle.' It was wide and low and spacious, as were all the affluent homes of that day, and now was ablaze with candles, to welcome the travellers. All along the streets friendly hands and kerchiefs had waved a welcome to us. Here, within, awaited a great gathering of family and friends, eager to see the chosen bride of a well-loved son.[6]

Clay Castle was to be their home during most of the next ten years and for considerable periods thereafter. Apparently, not until 1849 did they have a residence of their own; this was a summer cottage, near that of Clement's parents, on Monte Sano, a few miles east of Huntsville. Until Clement left the legislature in 1846, they returned periodically to Tuscaloosa where they resided with Virginia's relatives.

At the time of her marriage, Virginia's father-in-law owned three plantations and seventy slaves. Physically, life in his home must have been easy and comfortable for the daughter-in-law. But dwelling under the same roof with the Clays and their numerous kin must have required considerable mental and emotional adjustment for a person like Virginia whose zestfulness had been given relatively free play by the peculiar circumstances of her upbringing. The Clays were a closely knit clan, headed by a father who was characterized as "stern, and unbending." His wife, Susanna, was also a strong-minded person who not only supervised a large household but played an important part in running the Clay plantations. Surviving correspondence indicates the existence of affectionate relationships between Virginia and all her Clay connections, but these may have resulted largely from her yielding enough of her own individuality to be effectively absorbed into the family of her husband. Any anguish which may have accompanied the adjustment can only be surmised.

From the beginning, Virginia took a lively interest in her husband's career; Clement encouraged her interest, often consulting her about business and political activities. He did not stand for · reelection to the legislature in 1843, because he wanted to devote full time to law in a practice he shared with his father. Both father and son were Jacksonian Democrats and both went to Tennessee in 1844 to campaign for James Polk. At a Jackson birthday dinner in Huntsville on March 15, 1844, Clay junior paid a tribute to Old Hickory which did much to establish him as one of the state's most talented young orators. The favorable publicity contributed to his success when he finally sought reelection to the legislature in the summer of 1844.

In December 1844, Virginia accompanied her husband to Tuscaloosa for the opening of the legislative term. Shortly after arriving in the capital, she wrote her mother-in-law: *"The winter promises to be very gay*. The town is overflowing with strangers, and a great deal of visiting. To be in the parlour you might imagine me Miss T[unstall] again."[7]

Virginia took advantage of her popularity among the legislators to push her husband's candidacy in 1845 for the position of judge of the Madison County Court in Huntsville. Clay won the office but Virginia was stricken with a severe case of pneumonia, which her husband attributed to her overexertion in electioneering for him. For a while concern for her life was acute. Despite the cupping and blistering to which she was subjected by Tuscaloosa physicians, Virginia survived the illness. But her convalescence was so slow that her husband had to return to Huntsville without her at the end of the legislative session in February 1846. During the weeks of separation, Clement wrote affectionate letters to his ailing spouse. "Go to bed early," he admonished her on March 20. "Don't expose yourself to night air, in thin slippers, silk stockings, bare arms & neck, girded tight in the waist. . . . Be prudent, my dearest, in your words as well as acts. . . . You are so pretty & fascinating that I fear some fine looking fellow will forget you are a married woman & make love to you." On another occasion he wrote: "I fondly trust that when you return you will weigh 140 lbs & show no bone . . . about y[ou]r neck. And I do most earnestly beseech you to loosen your dresses. . . . even though y[ou]r waist grow as large as Sue McD's. I am not fond of wasp waists & I am very partial to fat ladies." Clement added that he hoped to increase his weight from 138 to 150 pounds and that he had "ceased using tobacco in every shape," with good results.[8]

Clay resigned his county judgeship in 1848 and did not seek political office for five years. During this period, he devoted himself mainly to practicing law, helping edit the Huntsville *Democrat*, which was controlled by the Clays and their kin, and to planting interests which involved the ownership of twenty-one slaves. He kept in close touch with political developments on both the local and national level, and moved more and more toward a Southern rights position as the controversy over the territories and slavery intensified. His abstention from officeseeking was due in large part to poor health. In the summer of 1850, accompanied by Virginia, he went to Philadelphia for medical treatment of his chronic cough. The doctors there sent him to a nearby beach, but when exposure to the sea atmosphere failed to bring relief he went to Brattleboro, Vermont, for futher treatment. His condition improved somewhat, but persistence of his respiratory troubles after return to Alabama sent him in February 1851 on another health-seeking jaunt, without Virginia. Two and one-half months of horseback riding in central Florida restored his strength and greatly improved his outlook on life.

In 1852 Virginia's health deteriorated to such an extent that she, in company with her brother-in-law, Hugh Lawson Clay, went to the Northeast for treatment. From Orange Mountain Water Cure, New Jersey, she wrote her husband on June 10: "I gave a plain statement of my case to Dr. Weder. He says my womb is displaced, by some means, but not so as to amount to falling but that it inclines to dragging on the left side, & that he can cure me he thinks. He tells me it may require 5 or 6 months. What do you think of that? I *cannot* stay so long without you. . . . My treatment at present is a half bath at six in the morning, foot [bath] at 11, sit[tin]g [bath?] at 4 & two injections daily with the curved tube vagina syringe. . . . There is a splendid bathing pool for the ladies, covered with an awning & I mean to learn to swim if possible." Ten days later she wrote: "My precious husband. . . . I feel & look improved & weigh 117 lbs & I hope to make 3 more pounds this month . . . & then if I don't gain 5 [more] lbs in August it will be because of a failure of the flour & beef markets. . . . I am trying to be economical but it is hard."9

Her sojourn in the East was saddened by news that the infant son of her brother-in-law, John Withers Clay, had died. "Now that

Death has entered our family," she wrote her husband on July 25, "I shall live in fear & trembling. Some way or other I have had more or less fear of a death than ever before in my life. If you or any grown member sh[oul]d sicken, do not fail to let us know instantly."[10]

Virginia did not remain under Dr. Weder's care as long as he had suggested. Instead, after a few weeks she went on for a short stay at the Brattleboro resort which she had visited with her husband two years before. En route she and "Brother Lawson" stopped overnight at Concord, New Hampshire, to see Franklin Pierce, the Democratic presidential candidate. Pierce had served in Congress with Virginia's father-in-law; all the Clays were supporting him in his bid for the Presidency. Despite a busy schedule, Pierce visited the Clays several times at their hotel and his wife once took Virginia for a carriage ride. Virginia, thrilled by this attention, wrote her husband that Pierce was "as fascinating & warm hearted as . . . a genuine southerner." Mrs. Pierce she described as "a pleasant, delicate, intellectual looking lady."[11]

Virginia rejoined her husband in Tuscaloosa in November 1852, just after Clement completed an intensive campaign in support of Pierce's candidacy. They must have enjoyed celebrating the Democratic triumph. A few months later, Clay launched a campaign to unseat the incumbent congressman from the Huntsville district, W.R.W. Cobb. Congressman Cobb was a man of limited education and unpolished manners, but he was a shrewd campaigner with a strong following among the white masses of North Alabama. Virginia accompanied her husband on his campaign and in one village, on an impulse, she persuaded the innkeeper's daughter to exchange her country sunbonnet for her own pretentious city-style hat. Henceforth, as she moved with her husband among his rural constitutents, her "pea-green cambric bonnet, lined with pink and stiffened with pasteboard slats" attracted much favorable attention. It proved what she later called "a political master-stroke" in that it helped Clay win a county that had previously been a Cobb stronghold. But Cobb, by making skillful use of Clay's secessionist leanings among a constituency that was overwhelmingly Unionist, carried all the district's other counties and decisively beat his opponent.[12]

The Clays were stronger in the state as a whole than they were in their own district. Later in 1853, when Clement made a bid for a seat in the United States Senate, the legislature rallied to his support and gave him an overwhelming majority.

On the trip to Washington in December 1853, the senator-elect and his wife traveled to Chattanooga by steamboat and proceeded thence by train to their destination. Among their fellow passengers were other members of the Alabama delegation, including W.R.W. Cobb, who teased Virginia about her sunbonnet escapade. She in turn chided him about singing his way to victory over her husband in the race for Congress. Cobb retorted: "You ought to feel obliged to me, for I made your husband a Senator."

On their arrival in Washington late at night, the clerk at the National Hotel, failing to recognize the weary and shabby-looking travelers, told them that there were no vacancies. Virginia, refusing to accept this pronouncement, walked to the desk and said: "I am Mrs. Clay of Alabama. You have refused my husband, Senator Clay and his friend, Representative Dowdell. What does it mean?" The embarrassed clerk quickly confessed his error and immediately escorted the party to their rooms.[13] After a short stay at the National, the Clays moved to a rooming house; in subsequent sessions they resided at other quarters including Brown's Hotel and the Ebbitt House. The move to Washington was one of the most important episodes in Virginia's life. For the first time in her career, she was on her own, so to speak, far removed from the well-meaning but overly protective scrutiny of her in-laws. As the wife of the youngest U. S. senator, who was himself the son of a senator and a member of one of Alabama's most influential families, she had entrée to the capital's elite. She combined the advantages accruing from her husband's background with her own considerable talent and charm to make new friendships and to win for herself and her spouse a position of solid respect among Washington's ruling elements on the eve of the Civil War.

During her first months in the capital, she suffered from poor health, culminating in the stillbirth of her only child. This sad experience forged a bond between her and Mrs. Pierce whose only surviving child, a little son, was killed in a railway accident just before she moved to the White House. Mrs. Pierce showed her friendly consideration for Virginia by taking her occasionally for a drive about the capital. Not until the fall of 1854 did Virginia emerge from her mourning and enter fully into the whirl of Washington life.

And a whirl it was, especially for young, ambitious, socially minded persons like the Clays. Official entertainments given by the President, cabinet members, foreign diplomats, and fellow members of Congress were interspersed by numerous private parties to provide what Mrs. Clay called "an unceasing . . . [and] augmenting round of dinners and dances, receptions and balls."[14]

Political notables and their wives with whom the Clays shared the many social events included the Howell Cobbs of Georgia, the James Chesnuts of South Carolina, Senator Thomas Hart Benton and his beautiful daughter Jesse of Missouri, and Supreme Court Justice and Mrs. John A. Campbell of Alabama. Among members of the House of Representatives set whose society Clement and Virginia enjoyed particularly were the L.Q.C. Lamars of Mississippi, the David Cloptons and the Phillip Phillipses of Alabama, and the Roger Pryors of Virginia. The Clays also made the acquaintance of Secretary of War Jefferson Davis and his wife Varina. Davis and Clay apparently were friendly from the time of their first meeting. Both were well-educated and studious, both suffered from chronic illness, and both were strongly committed to slavery and state's rights. Clay endeared himself to Davis by his solicitude for the Mississippian when the latter suffered the painful illness in 1858 which threatened to make him blind. "During that period," Mrs. Clay wrote in her memoir, "my husband gave up many nights to the nursing of the invalid who was tortured by neuralgic pains and nervous tension."[15] Clay further ingratiated himself with Davis when he used his good offices to help smooth over a misunderstanding between Davis and Judah P. Benjamin, a prominent lawyer-politician of Louisiana, following an angry verbal exchange on the Senate floor in June 1858. The friendship of their husbands drew the wives together and they saw enough of each other to develop a relationship of cordiality and mutual respect. The Davises evidenced their esteem by asking Clement to become the godfather of their son Joseph Evan Davis, born in Washington in 1859.

Most of the Clays' social intimates were Southerners. Exceptions were Senator and Mrs. George E. Pugh of Ohio. Concerning Mrs. Pugh, Virginia wrote: "[She] was something more than a woman of great personal loveliness. She was intellectual. . . . The bodily [beauty] so permeated by the spiritual, that she shone preeminent wherever she appeared, and this wholly independent of showy attire."[16]

Other feminine friends of the 1850s whom Virginia ranked near Mrs. Pugh in sparkle and charm were Adele Cutts who in 1856 became the second wife of Stephen A. Douglas, Mrs. Roger Pryor ("a perfect brunette . . . notable for . . . intellectuality"), and Mary Boykin Chesnut.[17]

In choosing her Washington friends, Virginia attached greatest importance to political influence, wealth, personal attractiveness, and sophistication. The women who impressed her most favorably were those who combined beauty with intellectuality.

Among the capital's richest hosts were the bankers, George W. Riggs and William W. Corcoran. The Clays were frequent guests at their sumptuous dinners and parties.

The White House was a relatively dull place during the Pierce administration. The situation changed with Buchanan's inauguration, and largely because of the sprightliness and charm of the venerable bachelor-president's hostess, his niece, Harriet Lane. Harriet and Virginia had much in common and became good friends.

The peak of Mrs. Clay's social activity in Washington came at a costume ball given in April 1858 by Senator and Mrs. William Gwin. At this affair Virginia portrayed ''Aunt Ruthy Partington,'' a rustic Yankee character created and made popular by a prominent humorist of the time, Benjamin P. Shillaber. She rehearsed the role so long and so diligently that she became expert in the twangy speech and ludicrous malapropisms for which ''the Widow Partington'' had become famous; and with the help of a theatrical makeup specialist, she achieved a disguise that deceived some of her closest friends. Mrs. Clay was the sensation of the evening. When she was presented to President Buchanan, she uninhibitedly exclaimed, ''Lor! Air you ralely 'Old Buck'? I've often heern tell o' Old Buck up in Beanville, but I don't see no horns!'' She sidled up to the British Ambassador, Lord Napier, and sympathetically inquired ''whether the Queen had got safely over her last encroachment.'' She took advantage of her disguise to chide Senator William H. Seward, whom she regarded as hostile to the South and had refused previously to meet. When Seward approached her and said, ''Aunt Ruthy, can't I, too, have the pleasure of welcoming you to the Federal City? May I have a pinch of snuff with you?'' Virginia gave him the snuff, but as she did so she told him that the snuff box had been given to her by the governor of Rhode Island, ''a lover of the Kawnstitution, Sir.''[18]

During their years in Washington the Clays occasionally attended plays and musical concerts. To supplement Washington entertainment and to replenish her wardrobe, Virginia made annual trips to New York. These trips caused concern over family finance, for Virginia liked fine clothes and good accommodations. The Clays, like most members of the antebellum South's ruling class, were well off in land and slaves, but they rarely were blessed with an amplitude of hard cash. However, their resources were sufficient to enable them between sessions to vacation at resorts on the Gulf Coast or in the highlands of the upper South. After a trip to Shocco Springs, North Carolina, in the fall of 1856, Virginia wrote her husband: "I found a great many pleasant friends . . . & was such a belle I was almost ashamed of it. I *fear* I shall be in the papers, in such brilliant colors, as will make me blush."[19] In the capital and on some of her travels, Virginia had the efficient assistance of a faithful Negro slave, Emily, for whom her husband had paid $1,600.

The Clays spent most of the congressional interlude of 1857 in Alabama working for Clement's reelection. Virginia assisted her husband in his campaigning. Their combined efforts resulted in the thwarting of all prospective contestants and in Clay's continuation in office.

In Washington, as in Alabama, Virginia did not hesitate to use her position as the wife of a powerful politician to seek favors for acquaintances and relatives.

Mrs. Clay and other congressional wives followed closely the political controversies in which their husbands were involved; and the growing acrimony of intersectional debate in House and Senate was paralleled and abetted by increasing tension in social circles. Washington society experienced a "cold war" in the 1850s, in which it appears that Southerners were the principal aggressors and that the women were greater haters than their husbands. This, at least, is the impression obtained from reading Mrs. Clay's letters and reminiscences. In December 1855, Virginia wrote her father-in-law from Mrs. Smith's boarding house: "We keep free-soilers, black Republicans & Bloomers the other side of the street."[20] She steadfastly refused her husband's pleas to let him introduce Senator Seward, and when someone at a private gathering brought up the prospect of attending a dinner to be given by another Northern senator, Mrs. Clay impetuously exclaimed: "Not even to save the Nation could I be induced to eat his bread, to drink his wine, to enter his domicile, to *speak* to him."[21]

Referring in her memoir to the months preceding secession, Mrs. Clay stated: "Not a Southern woman but felt with her husband, the stress of that session, [and] the sting of the wrongs the Southern faction of that great body was struggling to right." Virginia also recalled the North's "palpable envy of the hold the South had retained so long upon the Federal City, whether in politics or society."[22] Undoubtedly envy existed, but it was not confined to Northerners. The realities of the time and Virginia's reminiscent comments suggest that the greater envy was on the part of the Southerners. She referred repeatedly to the social predominancy of the Southerners in Washington, which she credited as lending "a charm to life in the Government circles of that day which lifted the capital to the very apex of its social glory."[23] She and other Southerners were greatly alarmed by evidence of the North's tremendous gains on the South in the 1850s, in population, wealth, and political power. The split of the Democratic party and the triumph of the Republicans in 1860 signified to the Clays, the Davises, the Chesnuts, and their kind, the end of Southern predominancy in national politics and in Washington society. The Southerners viewed those who supplanted them as their inferiors—socially, culturally, and politically, hostile to Southerners, and hell-bent on destroying slavery and the way of life which it represented. Clement Clay told a fellow Alabaman on November 15, 1860: "Of course we cannot live under the same government with those people unless we control it," and Jefferson Davis wrote Clay on January 19, 1861: "We have piped and they would not dance and now the devil may care."[24] Little wonder that congressmen of the deep South as early as December 13, 1860, in a joint communication, urged their constituents to disregard compromise proposals and sever relations with the Union.[25] Their wives wholeheartedly supported this action. When secession became a reality and Southern leaders in January rose one after another to give their valedictories in the Senate, women sitting in the gallery, according to Mrs. Clay who was there, "grew hysterical and waved their handkerchiefs, encouraging them with cries of sympathy and admiration." But their emotional displays did not betoken undiluted joy. Mrs. Clay, among others, sensed that the exodus from Washington meant the close of the grandest era of her long career. Looking back on her husband's farewell speech in the Senate after an interval of more than forty years, she spoke of the occasion as "surely the saddest day of my life."[26]

When Clay took his leave of the Senate on January 21, 1861, he had been suffering greatly from asthma for nearly a year. He had hardly begun his journey southward in February when he became so ill that he had to stop in Petersburg, Virginia, for treatment by his cousin, Dr. Thomas Withers. On Withers' recommendation, he and Virginia went to Minnesota where they remained about two months. The change of climate, quietude, and rest brought improvement in Clement's health; in late April he and Virginia returned to Huntsville. On May 10 Clement received a warm letter from Varina Davis inviting him and Virginia to Montgomery for a visit. "Time has not cooled the affectionate gratitude I feel for all your sympathy during Mr. Davis' illness, to me the darkest hour of my life," wrote Varina. "Mrs. Clay would enjoy seeing the many friends and acquaintances she has here."[27] Both the Clays, and especially Virginia, must have been thrilled by the thought of renewing old acquaintances as guests of the Confederate President. But Clay's health took a turn for the worse after he returned to Huntsville from Minnesota, and instead of going to Montgomery he and Virginia went to their summer cottage at Monte Sano. From there Virginia, on July 14, wrote her sister-in-law: "[My husband] had a bad night—took chloroform, & is wretched from it. Oh! My dear sister! You do not know how miserable I am. I fear the Mt. a failure & know not where else to go. I say nothing, do nothing towards a change, for fear of the worse."[28]

Virginia's anxiety for her husband was intensified by the gnawing fear that he might be suffering from tuberculosis. She found some diversion from reading the newspapers and corresponding with relatives including Hugh Lawson Clay, who went into the army and became adjutant general to E. Kirby Smith. Over the years she had developed a great affection for Lawson, whom she sometimes addressed as ''my own dear precious brother.'' On July 28, 1861, she wrote him: ''The only happy moment I have experienced since this war commenced was when the glad tidings came of the great victory of the South in the battles at Bull Run. My consistent prayer is that they may ever be victorious.''[29]

The coming of autumn brought a favorable turn in Clement's health and, as he grew strong in body, his mind turned increasingly to politics. In late October, with many affectionate admonitions from Virginia concerning rest and nourishment, he headed for Montgomery to campaign for a seat in the Confederate Senate. He triumphed over Thomas H. Watts by a vote of 66 to 53. In a subsequent drawing of lots to determine which senators should have two-, four-, and six-year terms, Clement's term was fixed at two years.

Early in February 1862, he and Virginia proceeded to Richmond, where they moved into a rooming house run by Mrs. Duval. He was sworn in as senator on February 19. Three days later, he and his fellow legislators and a large group of citizens, which must have included Virginia, braved a heavy rain to witness the inauguration of Jefferson Davis as President under the permanent Confederate constitution. During his two years as senator, Clay worked hard and won the respect of his colleagues, half of whom had served in the Federal Congress. He generally supported the Davis administration, but he sponsored no major law and he deserves to be rated as a good senator rather than a great one.

Because of congestion and the high cost of living in Richmond, Clay resided there only when Congress was in session. This meant that he lived in the Confederate capital for only about forty-two weeks during his two years as senator. Virginia was with him for only about twenty-five of those weeks; the rest of the time she stayed with relatives in North Carolina, Georgia, and South Carolina.

Mrs. Clay's circle of friends in Richmond consisted largely of Southern political and military leaders and their wives whom she and her husband had known in Washington. Among them were the Jefferson Davises, the James Chesnuts, Senator and Mrs. Thomas J. Semmes of Louisiana and Mrs. Louis T. Wigfall of Texas, Secretary of the Navy Stephen R. Mallory and his wife, Colonel and Mrs. L.Q.C. Lamar, and General and Mrs. Joseph E. Johnston. Friends among the capital's younger set were Burton Harrison, an aide to President Davis, and his beautiful sweetheart, Constance Cary, General J.E.B. Stuart, and General John Bell Hood. But for a number of reasons, including shortage of money, lack of facilities for entertaining, and the brevity of her stays in the Southern capital, Virginia did not lead as active a social life in Richmond as in Washington.

Her greatest social triumph in Richmond was her performance as Mrs. Malaprop in an amateur production of Sheridan's "Rivals," staged at the spacious home of Mrs. Joseph C. Ives, whose husband was a colonel on the staff of President Davis. About three hundred guests witnessed the performance, among them the Jefferson Davises and numerous other high-ranking members of the political and military establishment. The cast of characters included Constance Cary as Lydia Languish, and Virginia's beautiful sister-in-law, Celeste, as Lydia's maid, Lucy. Virginia, whose elaborate makeup included a coiffure heightened by piling false hair on top of a pair of black satin boots, was the hit of the show. Mrs. Chesnut, who witnessed the performance, wrote in her diary: "Mrs. Clay as Mrs. Malaprop was beyond our wildest hopes, and she was in such earnest when she pinched (Connie Cary) Lydia Languish'[s] shoulder and called her 'an antricate little huzzy' [that] Lydia showed she felt it and the next day was black and blue. [Even] the back of Mrs. Clay's head was eloquent."[30] Forty years later, Mrs. Ives wrote Virginia: "You carried the audience by storm. . . . I can see you yet, in imagination, in your rich brocaded gown, antique laces and jewels, high puffed and curled hair, with nodding plumes which seemed to add expression to your amusing utterances!"[31]

Throughout their residence in Richmond, the Clays were harassed by worry over affairs in Alabama. On April 11, 1862, near the end of Clement's first session in the Senate, Federal forces occupied Huntsville. They left after five months because of General Braxton Bragg's movement into Kentucky. But they came back in July 1863, and were either in the area or threatening it for the remainder of the war. Twice the invaders arrested Clement's father, who was then in his seventies and broken in health. Management of the plantations fell largely on his wife, Susanna, aided by her daughter-in-law, Mary, the wife of John Withers Clay, who after the initial Federal invasion became an itinerant newspaper editor in Confederate-controlled portions of Tennessee and Georgia. Susanna's difficulties were greatly complicated by depradations of the Federal forces and the demoralizing effects of their presence on the Negro slaves. In occasional letters smuggled through Yankee lines, Susanna told Clement and Virginia of her troubles. "We cannot exert any authority," she wrote in the summer of 1863, "y[ou]r Negroes are free as ours. Where masters are [present] they do better— but all . . . expect that all the Negroes able to go will do so when the cars run or the Y[ankee]s get here."[32] On the trip that Clement was able to make to Huntsville, late in 1862, he hired some of the Negroes out to operators of niter caves near the town, but later, after the return of the Union troops, many of the blacks ran away and those who stayed home were under little control. Early in 1864 Clay was informed: "Y[ou]r negroes on Mt. Sano have declared their freedom, occupy y[ou]r mountain home, sleep in y[ou]r bed & sheets—use y[ou]r china &c. . . . On a visit from y[ou]r mother . . . she was . . . told she need give no more orders to them."[33]

Clement and Virginia accepted their misfortunes with considerable equanimity. Their childlessness gave them mobility and they benefited from the hospitality and help of numerous well-fixed relatives. On May 29, 1862, Clement wrote from the home of his Comer relatives in Macon, Georgia, to Virginia who was visiting her uncle, Buxton Williams: "I am sure that my kin here will welcome you with open arms & share their plenty with us most gladly; & as we are exiles from home I prefer feeding on y[ou]r or my kin to accepting the hospitality of strangers."[34] The travel incident to moving about among relatives and shifting from the deep South to Richmond and back involved considerable discomfort, owing to crowded trains, irregular schedules, and poor accommodations at stopovers along the way. After a trip from North Alabama to Macon in January 1863, Virginia wrote Clement and his parents:

> I was sick all Sat[urday] night, Sunday and Sunday night with a violent attack of cholera morbus. . . . I think it was induced by our diet on the way & cold taken at Atlanta. . . . We fumigated the room at Atlanta. . . . Fearing robbery by chloroform I slept with *all* the money in one *stocking* & mine & Alice's watches, chatelaines & pins in the other. . . . We slept three in a bed. . . . We rode from Stevenson to Chattanooga in the freight train, the baggage cars or the passenger being unable to receive a single trunk. Arriving at C[hattanooga] we w[oul]d have been forced to go to a smallpox hotel or [re]main in the streets, but for the gallan[try] of an . . . officer of Washington memory who g[ave] his room, beds, &c.[35]

The anxieties and inconveniences resulting from the war deepened the affection between Virginia and her husband. This is indicated by the correspondence during their first lengthy period of separation, January-April 1863, when he was in Richmond and she was staying with her sister-in-law, Celeste Clay, and Celeste's parents, the Comers, in Macon, Georgia. She addressed him as "My dear dearest" and "My own precious husband." She sent him handkerchiefs, toilet articles, shirts, and a robe which she made from a discarded dress. She once expressed pleasure that he was "having a good time" from liquor that she had provided. She repeatedly admonished him not to neglect his health and his appearance. On February 24, 1863, she wrote: "Do dress like a gentleman, & a senator, my darling, for *my* sake. Strangers, by scores, who do not *know* you, see you. Comb y[ou]r hair & beard & use clean fresh hand[kerchie]fs, won't you? You look old & dilapidated when you neglect yourself."[36]

Clement's letters to Virginia overflowed with affection. She was especially pleased by those he wrote her on her thirty-eighth birthday, January 16, 1863, and their twentieth wedding anniversary two weeks later. In response to the first she wrote: "My birthday epistle entirely reconciles me to my *age* wh[ich] fact proves you a great orator on paper as well as in speech. . . . I cannot write you my darling how y[ou]r tenderness & love overwhelmed me. I . . . will try to prove my own for you in my life time devotion."[37]

The one discordant note sounded by Virginia during this affectionate exchange was caused by her suspicion that Clement was remiss in completing arrangements that would enable her to join him in Richmond. Hugh Lawson Clay, who was sharing Clement's room and bed at Mrs. Duval's, seemed also to blow hot and then cold about having his Celeste accompany Virginia to Richmond. On February 14, 1863, Virginia wrote petulantly: "If you & bro[ther] L[awson] are really desirous & *prefer* we sho[uld] remain here for *one* or *six* months—just *say so*, as you sh[oul]d to *grown-up, sensible people* & not be any more attempting to beguile or deceive us like silly children into y[ou]r wishes."[38]

One of the reasons for Virginia's impatience to get to Richmond was a desire to see her cousin, Tom Tunstall, who had gone into

Yankeedom to buy articles scarce or unobtainable in the Confederacy—including some fine clothes for Virginia—and who was expected to return soon. She was also eager to obtain some finery due for delivery in Richmond from Paris. These purchases were a severe strain on Clement's already limited resources. Shortage of money was partly responsible for his lack of enthusiasm in advising his wife to join him in Richmond. "Our board is very high," he wrote his mother on February 18, 1863, "& when our wives come will exceed our pay." Three weeks later, in reply to her letter in which she had added a three-word postscript, "Money, money, money," Clement wrote: "I send you one Hundred Dollars in this, all the money I have. Do economize, as we have nothing that we can rely on now but my salary. . . . I am . . . more pinched than I would be in consequence of advancing $700 for Tom T[unstall] of wh[ich] I borrowed $400 at 12 per cent interest, to be repaid next month." The dismal tone of this letter was relieved a bit by Clay's teasing reference to his wife's weight. "I am rejoiced to hear from Col. S.," he stated, "that you weigh 155 pounds, are a *great* belle (of course, if weighing 155) & are enjoy[in]g y[ou]r self very much." A few days later he informed Virginia that Tom Tunstall had ventured into Washington, against Clay's earnest admonition, and had been captured. But he added that Tom, before his capture, had sent a few articles to Richmond for Virginia, "some . . . gaiters . . . some handkerch[ie]fs & stockings & a fine hair brush & gauntlets, all very nice."[39]

In response to Clement's urge to economize, Virginia wrote on March 19, 1863: "I am much obliged for . . . the advice. . . . I will try but you know my blood." She told him that she and Celeste, "two poor widows," were "trying in vain to solace each other." She added the very touching statement: "In truth my darling my heart is almost starving for a little love and I am almost forced to concede y[ou]r oft repeated assertion that I c[oul]d not live a widow if I *would*. . . . Loula came yes[terday]. . . . Her children are splendid & she has made L[estia] & myself more baby crazy

**Virginia Tunstall (later Mrs. C. C. Clay, Jr.) with two of
her Tunstall kin. Photo taken shortly before her marriage to C. C. Clay, Jr.**

Courtesy of Duke University Library

Mrs. Clement C. Clay, Jr.

(From Ada Sterling, ed., A Belle of the Fifties, New York, Doubleday, Page & Company, 1904.)

Mrs. Clement C. Clay, Jr.
Date and place of photo unknown.

Courtesy of Duke University Library

Jefferson Davis and C. C. Clay, Jr.
Photo taken between 1871 and 1875, probably on one of
Davis's visits to Huntsville, Alabama. (See Ruth K.
Nuermberger, *The Clays of Alabama*, **p. 312.)**

Courtesy of Duke University Library

Mrs. Virginia Clay-Clopton, formerly Mrs. C. C. Clay, Jr., at about age 90.
Probably taken when she celebrated her 90th birthday in Huntsville, January 16, 1915. (See Ruth K. Nuermberger, *The Clays of Alabama*, p. 318.)

than ever. I fear th[at] nothing will come of it—however, we'll see.''⁴⁰

Apparently, Virginia and Celeste were able to join their husbands in Richmond shortly before the third session of Congress adjourned on May 1, 1863. Virginia must have made a special effort to see the Davises, for during the early months of 1863, relations between the President and Clay had become decidedly cool. This was disturbing to the Clays, especially to Virginia, who had requested Clement on March 19 to deliver to the President ''an old maid's mat'' which she had made for him, and to ''say a great many kind & sweet things to him for me.'' She expressed concern about newspaper reports of Davis' failing eyesight and poor health, and added: ''I think with mother that 'he is a great & goodman' & I believe that God will yet preserve him to *see* the land and the people who owe him so much, free and happy.''⁴¹

The circumstances of the Clay-Davis rupture in 1863 were similar to those of the Chesnut-Davis estrangement in 1861, except that the principals in 1863 were the men instead of the women. Clay first informed Virginia of the unfortunate situation when he wrote her on March 12, 1863: ''He [Davis] has not been so cordial with me, or so free or confiding, since my arrival [in January], as to make me feel disposed to use my old conclusion 'y[ou]r true friend'. We have had no quarrel or difference, only a growing indifference & coldness that has prevented my visiting him more than 4 or 5 times since I reached here.'' Clement added that he would withhold delivering the mats that she had made for the President until he got from her a letter to take along with them. ''Write your prettiest letter,'' he advised, ''as *warm* as you please & say to him that you had hoped & expected to deliver the mats in person.'' On March 20, Clay wrote Virginia: ''I handed the mats & y[ou]r letter to the Pres[i]d[en]t. He read it & remarked 'she says not a word of coming here. Am I not to have the pleasure of seeing her this session? Give her my love when you write'.''⁴²

Despite this show of cordiality, relations between Davis and

Clay grew worse. One cause was the President's great strain over the deteriorating military situation, especially in Mississippi. Another was Clay's close association with some of the President's chief enemies, including Senators Louis T. Wigfall and William L. Yancey. In April 1862, Clay and Yancey had written Davis a letter pointing out that Alabama did not have brigadiers in numbers commensurate with the regiments the state had contributed to Confederate service, and asking for promotion of four Alabama colonels. Davis rejected the proposal with a brusque statement, reminding the senators that nomination of officers was a presidential prerogative. Yancey was deeply offended and so informed Davis. Controversy flared up again in April 1863, when Clay and Yancey proposed appointment of one Glackmeyer as postmaster at Montgomery, and Davis instead nominated E. M. Burton. Clay called on the President in an endeavor to persuade him to accept his and Yancey's candidate, but to no avail. On May 2 Clay reported the interview to Yancey, who had returned to Alabama: "I told him I would not vote for B[urton]. He said: 'Very well. If you think it right to object to a good man because you and your colleague preferred another, do so.' I said: 'I think the Senate will reject him.' *Whereupon* he became excited and vehement—Said the Senate could not dragoon him into nominating their choice, etc. etc. I left him in a bad humor with you Chilton and myself." Clay added: "Some of my friends think he [Davis] will show his friendship to [me] by trying to have me defeated next fall if I run for the Senate." There is no indication that Davis took any such action. Yancey's death on July 27, 1863, removed a principal source of friction between Clement and the President. And, too, Virginia may have written soothing letters to the Confederate White House in an effort to restore good relations.[43]

Virginia and Clement spent most of the summer and fall of 1863 with relatives in Georgia. In August Clay went alone to Montgomery to take part in political maneuvering that resulted in the election of Robert Jemison as Yancey's successor in the Confederate Senate. He went back in November in a desperate effort to win his own reelection. Interestingly, an argument used against him, with considerable effect, was his consistent support of the Davis administration. Perhaps the greatest obstacle to his reelection was his vote against a bill to raise the pay of Confederate soldiers. Clay justified his opposition to the measure on the grounds that it was inflationary, but his action unquestionably alienated many of his erstwhile supporters. The humiliation of his defeat and his lame duck status must have cast a pall over their life in Richmond during his final session in Congress, December 7, 1863-February 17, 1864. He devoted considerable thought and effort to finding new employment. He even talked about enlisting in the army as a private, but it is difficult to believe that he seriously contemplated such a lowly and unremunerative position.[44]

President Davis came to his rescue in late April 1864, by appointing him special emissary to Canada, along with Jacob Thompson and James P. Holcombe, to promote Confederate interests in the British colony and to encourage resistance to the Union government in the country south of the Canadian border. The presidential appointment signified that the antipathy which had flared up the previous year had abated. An important factor in that reconciliation was the death of Clay's godson, Joseph Evan Davis, from a fall at the Confederate White House on April 30, 1864. Both Clement and Virginia wrote the stricken parents tender letters of condolence in which they expressed deep appreciation of past friendship and kindnesses.

On May 6 Clay ran the blockade out of Wilmington and sailed for Bermuda where he boarded a ship for Halifax. After a three-week delay there from illness, he proceeded to Montreal, arriving at that city on June 11, 1864. He was destined to remain in Canada for more than eight months on a mission that accomplished very little. In slipping back into the Confederacy on February 2, 1865, his ship ran aground off Charleston; he lost most of his baggage and had to wade ashore.

Virginia had considered accompanying her husband to Canada, but the peril of running the blockade, and uncertainties about conditions of residence abroad, resulted in her reluctant decision to remain in the Confederacy. After bidding Clement a fond farewell in Petersburg on April 30, 1864, she stayed in that city for a week with his cousin, Dr. John Withers. Reports of the proximity of the Federals caused her on May 7 to head southward. After visiting Georgia relatives, she moved in October to the home of Celeste's sister, Loula, wife of Paul Hammond, son of former U.S. Senator James H. Hammond of South Carolina. Loula and Paul occupied the James Hammond estate, Redcliffe, located on Beach Island in the Savannah River near Augusta, Georgia. Paul, a captain in the Confederate army, was frequently absent, and the two women spent much time on the plantation alone, save for the presence of the Hammond slaves.

Redcliffe was a beautiful place, and its fields, forests, and streams yielded an abundance and variety of food. Virginia suffered little if any physical discomfort during her four months' residence with the congenial and hospitable Loula.

With the threat of Sherman's invasion, Virginia moved in late January 1865 to Macon where she remained until her husband rejoined her on February 10.

Despite the kindness of relatives and friends, Virginia suffered much anguish of spirit during the long separation from her husband. On November 18, 1864, she wrote him plaintively: "The 'Violette [Virtue?] Contract' [that we made when you left for Canada] so far a failure—*waiting for you. I intend to sue for damages.*"[45]

The pain of separation was aggravated by concern for Clement's health, uncertainty about the time of his return, and fear that he would be captured, injured, or killed as he tried to make his way back through the ever-tightening blockade. Communication with her husband was sparse and uncertain, and was conducted partly through "personals" inserted in a friendly newspaper, the New

York *News*. In mid-November Virginia wrote Clement: "It gives me great pain to learn that none of my numerous letters have reached you since 30th June! I have sent you dozens, my dearest, filled with . . . more love than ever filled my heart before the noblest of men & best of husbands." She also thanked him for "package and Fans" recently received and repeated a request made in many previous communications that he bring her "some pretty things" including two silk dresses, six French corsets 22 inches in the waist, cotton hose, size 9, "some slippers, with heels No. 3-1/2," two dozen gloves and a dozen dark handkerchiefs. "If French importations are to be had," she stated, "bring me a spring bonnet & a walking hat, for the benefit of all my lady friends, as well as myself." She also asked him to bring some fine dresses and furs for Celeste and Loula. Clement faithfully made a list of all these items, but if he succeeded in acquiring them, they were lost when his ship ran aground at Charleston.[46]

Their reunion at Macon on February 10 must have been a joyful occasion. But happiness was diluted by the widespread disruption and demoralization that presaged Confederate defeat. A week after their reunion, they headed toward Richmond so that Clay could make a final report on his activities in Canada. Virginia accompanied him only as far as Washington, Georgia, where they remained about a month as guests of Robert Toombs, while Clement recovered from an illness that befell him along the way. On March 25, he resumed his journey, leaving Virginia in Georgia. He reached Richmond on Sunday afternoon, April 2, made a report to Secretary of State Judah P. Benjamin, and then called on Jefferson Davis who was deeply involved in getting his papers and belongings ready for a hasty departure from the Confederate capital. Clay accompanied the presidential party to Danville, Virginia, and a few days later headed for Georgia. En route he learned of Lee's surrender and the assassination of Abraham Lincoln. After rejoining Virginia late in April, he proceeded with her to the home of Senator Benjamin H. Hill of LaGrange, Georgia. There he learned from a newspaper report that Federal authorities in Washington had charged him, Jefferson Davis, and Jacob Thompson with involvement in Lincoln's assassination, and had offered $100,000 reward for their arrest. After an anxious consultation with Virginia and with friends who had assembled at the Hill mansion, Clay telegraphed James H. Wilson, the Union general in command at Macon, his intention to turn himself in. Virginia was almost beside herself with fear as she accompanied her husband to Macon, despite certainty that he was wholly innocent of complicity in Lincoln's murder. At Macon, they joined the recently captured Jefferson Davis, and by train and boat proceeded with him, his family, and other Confederate notables—all under Federal military escort—to Hilton Head, South Carolina. There on May 15 the party was put on board the steamship *William P. Clyde* and sent on their way to Fort Monroe. During the four-day voyage Virginia suffered from illness brought on by a combination of the rolling sea and chronic worry. In a diary that she kept during this period, she noted: "My darling keeps well and is calm and heroic. . . . My heart palpitates with fear."[47]

The ship dropped anchor off Fort Monroe on May 20. Three days later Federal soldiers and "two Yankee women" came aboard and subjected the Southerners and their baggage to a thorough search, after which Davis and Clay were removed to Fort Monroe for imprisonment. Virginia wrote in her diary: "Oh GOD what a blow! Farewell."[48]

The next day Virginia, Varina, and the Davis children headed south and after a stormy and miserable voyage, reached Savannah on May 28. Following a visit of two weeks in that city, during which the elite of the community showered her with kindnesses, Virginia visited relatives in Augusta and Macon. In August she returned to Huntsville where she found a situation vastly different from that which she had left nearly three years before. Her parents-in-law were now old and feeble (both were to die in 1866). Her brothers-in-law had despaired of running the plantations with free Negro labor. John Withers Clay's wife, Mary, was making a little money teaching. The Freedmen's Bureau had taken over Clement's office. Virginia tried to collect some debts but without success. She met her daily needs by drawing on a small hoard of gold left from the war; money required for extraordinary expenses such as travel was obtained by borrowing.

The eleven months of Clement's imprisonment brought out, in a degree unmatched previously or afterward, the better aspects of Virginia's personality and character. Her life was dominated by one central purpose: to obtain her husband's freedom. Pursuit of that objective stimulated her energies to an unprecedented extent, took her mind off herself, released her from the narrow confines of public activity to which members of her sex normally were restricted, and made her a relatively liberated woman.

Her first step was a letter-writing campaign on behalf of her husband, which she initiated as early as the voyage from Fort Monroe to Savannah and continued throughout the summer and fall. Directly or indirectly, she communicated with prominent lawyers, journalists, and political leaders of Washington, New York, Boston, and other Northern cities, many of them friends of prewar years whom she considered well disposed toward her husband. Friendly letters came from Franklin Pierce, Duff Green, and numerous others, emphatically stating their confidence in Clay's innocence and pledging their willingness to render all possible assistance in obtaining his freedom. Richard J. Haldeman, a Pennsylvania friend, wrote on July 24, 1865, that he had talked with Congressman Thaddeus Stevens about Clay and that "Mr. Stevens scorned the idea of either his guilt or that of any of the prominent sojourners in Canada."[49]

On September 16, 1865, Virginia wrote President Andrew Johnson a long letter pleading Clay's innocence of "the heinous crime imputed to him" and asking for permission to visit her husband. "As a daughter of the South & the wife of y[ou]r noble prisoner," she wrote, "I implore you to grant this appeal of an

agonized woman: Say that I can see my husband . . . or give me one
hope of his release & I will fly to you, with words & tears of
grateful thanks for y[ou]r justice, magnanimity & clemency."[50]

When the letter brought no response, Virginia got Duff Green's
son, Ben, to see if it had been delivered at the White House. Ben
informed her that it had been delivered, but that Johnson had taken
no action on it. "My advice," Green stated, "is to come on at once
& see the President in person. . . . 'Tis said that . . . he don't like
intermediaries and that the ladies never fail with him."[51]

Virginia acted quickly. With a new dress and a hundred dollars
provided by a Huntsville merchant, she departed for Washington
in mid-November. On arrival she checked in at the Willard Hotel,
made contact with many old friends, and asked for an appointment
with the President. While waiting a reply she conferred with
several prominent Washingtonians, among them Ulysses S.
Grant. General Grant graciously wrote a note to the President in
which he stated: "The manner of Mr. Clay's surrender I think is a
full guarantee that if released on parole to appear when called for
. . . he will be forthcoming. . . . I respectfully recommend that C.
C. Clay, now a State prisoner, be released on parole."[52]

On her visit to the White House on November 22, 1865, Virginia was accompanied by the widow of Stephen A. Douglas.
When the President seemed unmoved by Mrs. Clay's earnest pleas
on her husband's behalf, Mrs. Douglas fell weeping to her knees
and urged her companion to follow her example. But Virginia was
too proud to prostrate herself before one for whom she had as much
distaste as Andy Johnson. A visit to Stanton's office proved as
futile as the call on the President, though her reception by that
awesome dignitary was far more considerate than she had anticipated.

While awaiting action from the White House, Virginia made a
ten-day trip to New York where she conferred with several sympathetic notables, including Horace Greeley. When she returned to

Washington, she reported to her parents-in-law: "Hospitalities without number proffered. And, will you believe it, thousands of dollars." At the same time she wrote her husband expressing her disappointment at her failure to make more progress toward obtaining his release; but she added: "I am *very hopeful* still my darling & will you know leave no avenue of assistance untried."[53]

In this letter, as in many others written during the long imprisonment, Virginia took great pain to keep up her husband's spirit, for she was fully aware of the close relationship between his morale and his physical well-being. She represented home conditions as favorably as she could, told him of her devotion to his aged parents, reassured him often of her deep and abiding affection, played down her own anxieties and difficulties, urged him to keep up his hopes, and importuned him to guard his health. She advised him to turn to the Bible for spiritual consolation and pledged to him the continuing prayers of family and friends for his preservation and release.

Late in December 1865, after many visits to the White House and some sharp verbal exchanges with Andrew Johnson, in which Virginia manifested more spunk than tact, she finally received the President's permission to visit Clement at Fort Monroe. Following her arrival, she had to wait a full day while the officer in command, General Nelson A. Miles, telegraphed Secretary of War Stanton for approval of Johnson's order authorizing the visit. The couple were allowed only one evening together, but the actuality of reunion after seven months of separation must have brought great comfort to both.

Virginia was shocked by Clement's haggard appearance and desolate spirit. Shortly after her return to Washington, she wrote the President on January 11, 1866: "Mr. Clay, always delicate, is dying daily. His thin, pale face daggered my heart to look upon! He told me he was dying, but resigned. . . . Mr. President, I am . . . without parents, brother, sister, or child. My husband is my

treasure, my world, my all. . . . Give him to me for a little while, at
least. . . . Give him the parole I ask & then 'if he perish, he will
perish'."[54]

Johnson did not grant Virginia's request for an immediate
parole, but authorized her to visit Clement as often as she wished.
She went back to Fort Monroe late in January 1866 for a second
and longer visit, after which she intensified her efforts to pressure
the Chief Executive into releasing her husband. She bombarded
Johnson with notes, made frequent visits to the White House, and
entreated others to petition the President on Clement's behalf.
Congressman Thaddeus Stevens, Senator Henry Wilson, and
former Secretary of the Treasury Robert J. Walker responded with
heartening recommendations of Clay's parole. These activities
reached a climax near midnight of April 17, when Virginia, after
waiting several hours at the White House, confronted the President
at his desk and addressed him with such force that he picked up his
pen and wrote an order for Clay's parole. On his release the next
day, Clement proceeded to Petersburg where Virginia shortly
joined him. After a few days of relaxation with their kin and
friends, they headed for Alabama. Their arrival in Huntsville on
April 29 was the occasion of a great celebration. In reporting the
homecoming, the Huntsville *Daily Independent* stated:

> We hardly expected to see him looking as well as he does.
> The trouble, harassment and deprivations of prison life have,
> however, left visible marks upon his frame, and his head is
> sprinkled with premature gray. . . . Mrs. Clay . . . is an equal
> sharer in the esteem and admiration that is so justly due her,
> not only for her unrivalled virtues and graces, but for that
> exalted womanly devotion which in the true heart is only the
> more developed and fixed when the trials of adversity en-
> compass us about. We wish them a long and joyous life after
> the eventful and discordant scenes through which they have
> passed.[55]

The joyous life which the editor invoked for Clement and Virginia did not materialize. Clay was harassed by debts dating back to prewar times, and these were only partly met by the sale of property that he and his brothers inherited when their father died in September 1866. Returns from his plantation, the sale of furniture, and various other expedients proved so meager that Clement in 1871 welcomed an opportunity to go into the insurance business. But this venture failed after two years, and Clay settled down in a cottage on his plantation eighteen miles from Huntsville. He had little talent for agricultural administration and he was handicapped by poor health. Economically, times were hard more often than they were good. The drabness of rural life was broken by occasional visits from friends including Jefferson Davis, and by periodic trips to Huntsville. Congress restored his citizenship in June 1880. He died on January 3, 1882, less than a month after his sixty-fifth birthday.

Virginia was frequently away from her husband during the fifteen years that he lived after getting out of prison. He had been her dominant interest during his confinement and working for his release had given her an all-absorbing purpose. But once he was free, and doomed by circumstances to a drab and secluded existence, she became dissatisfied and restless. She was too gregarious and too much of an activist to fold her hands and settle down resignedly to impecunious country life. Probably to relieve her boredom, though ostensibly to prevent confiscation of Clay's property, she and her husband made a trip to Washington and New York in 1866. After a little while Clement returned to Huntsville but Virginia lingered in the East until March 1867. During her visit in Washington, she obtained an order from Attorney General Henry Stanbery for release to Clement of Clay's office building in Huntsville that had been taken over in 1866 by the Freedmen's Bureau. On July 1, 1868, the day that Clay returned from two months of travel in Tennessee and Kentucky for his health, Virginia took off for New York to attend the Democratic Convention

and to visit friends in that city and in Washington. She did not
return to Alabama until the latter part of November. During her
five-month absence, Clay sought escape from his loneliness by
pottering about his country cottage, but with little success. In his
misery he wrote plaintively to Virginia: "I am trying to prepare our
log cabin for y[ou]r reception. . . . It if were possible for you to
love me & enjoy my company as I love you & enjoy y[ou]rs we
might be happy in our seclusion."[56]

But Virginia apparently found the seclusion of the plantation
uncongenial. She spent a substantial portion of her time during
1868-1882 in Huntsville, first in a boarding house and, after 1872,
in an apartment Clement provided for her in his old office building.
Clement shared these quarters with her when he came into town for
business or relaxation, and she occasionally went to the plantation
for various periods. She filled the role of hostess during Jefferson
Davis's visits to the plantation in the early 1870s. After one of
these visits, Davis wrote Virginia: "How often have I recalled the
happy hours . . . around your broad chimney place, with its
grandly hospitable fire."[57]

Whenever she could, Virginia abandoned the dreary atmosphere of North Alabama to visit friends in Memphis. In the gay
surroundings of that city she danced, dined, went to the theater,
and recaptured for a time the glamorous existence of prewar years.
During one of these trips she wrote Clement: "I am more than ever
disenchanted of H[untsville]. Memphis was never so gay outdoors
as this past week. Two great theatrical attractions—four grand
Festivals for churches . . . & cars running with flags flying make it
very gay."[58] Such communications must have been hard on
Clement's morale. Once when he wrote of his unhappy plight she
replied: "I feel lonely & sad & poor, miserably enough be sure,
tho' I try to smile thro[ugh] it all. When I see the luxurious homes
of the Parkers & Bartletts & trousseaux from Paris, & think of my
lot, my home & my one black silk dress,—I do not need in addition

one word from you or any other one to realize my situation.''[59]
This pointed reminder of her husband's failure to give her the sort
of life she had known in better days must have cut him deeply.

After Clement's death in 1882, Virginia had to move to the
plantation. During her latter years she shared the plantation dwelling, to which she gave the name Wildwood, with two orphaned
nieces of her favorite cousin, Tom Tait Tunstall. In 1884 she made
her one and only trip to Europe as the chaperone of two young
cousins, Fannie Tunstall and Mary Dearing. She spent a portion of
the winter of 1885-1886 in Washington where she was a much
admired participant in the capital's choicest social activities.

In November 1887, Virginia, then sixty-two, married David
Clopton, a justice of the Alabama Supreme Court, aged sixty-
seven. The twice-widowered judge had been Clay's colleague in
both the Federal and Confederate Congresses, and a close friendship had developed between the two families during that association. Clopton's distinguished background and high standing, together with Virginia's continuing sprightliness and charm, gave
her a conspicuous role in Montgomery society during the four
years of her second marriage. After Clopton's death in February
1892, Virginia took the hyphenated name, Clay-Clopton, and
moved back to the plantation cottage in which Clay had spent his
last years. There, despite limited means and advancing years, she
enjoyed a varied and active life. She worked for woman's suffrage, wrote articles for magazines and newspapers, attended
reunions of Confederate veterans, and served as honorary life
president of the United Daughters of the Confederacy. She also
worked intermittently on her memoirs with the considerable help
of Ada Sterling, an experienced New York journalist who spent
several months in Virginia's home. The reminiscences were published in 1904 under the title *A Belle of the Fifties*.

On January 16, 1915, Virginia, ''gowned in black velvet and
duchess lace'' and wearing a large corsage of pink roses, cele-

brated her ninetieth birthday at a grand party given by a Huntsville friend. She died six months later on June 23, 1915, after a brief illness.[60]

What kind of a person was Virginia Tunstall Clay-Clopton? One of her greatest weaknesses was an undue concern for material things. In 1852 she wrote her husband: "Do you often go to see Mary Ewing? Go often, first from a feeling of kindness towards a miserable girl . . . & 2nd it may be of benefit to you in a monied way."[61] Four years later she wrote a young relative who was in the consular service in Spain: "Don't wed abroad coz unless you are *sure* of a half a million at least; if she has that you may go ahead."[62] In her memoirs she quotes Mrs. John J. Crittenden's comment on that lady's three marriages: "My first marriage was for love, and it was mine as fully as I could wish; my second for money, and Heaven was good to me in this instance; my third was for position, and that too, is mine. What more could I ask?" Mrs. Clay adds significantly: "What more, indeed!"[63]

She was proud, vain, and snobbish. She felt a strong attachment to her kin and she regarded the blood that coursed through their veins and hers as the best in the nation. In reporting to her cousin Tom Tunstall the very special attentions shown her by President Pierce's wife in 1856, she stated: "But you know we are a rare people and fit for the company of the highest people in the land."[64] After a visit from another cousin early in 1865, she noted in her diary: "He is a true son of the blood & dear to my heart."[65] Referring in her memoirs to the plebeian ways of one of her husband's rustic political opponents, she stated: "These evidences of his democracy gave huge delight to the masses, though it aroused in me, a young wife, great indignation that in the exigencies of a public career my husband should be compelled to enter a contest with such a man. To me it was the meeting of a Damascus blade and a meat-axe, and in my soul I resented it."[66] She wrote condescendingly of unaristocratic constituents who occasionally came to Washington expecting to be entertained by her husband and his well-born colleagues. Of the circle in which she moved during the years in Washington, she wrote: "They were a rich and exclusive . . . class."[67] She devoted page after page to descriptions of their lofty status, their elegant appearance, their luxurious dwellings, and their sumptuous parties. Her vanity crops up repeatedly in references, both in her reminiscences and letters, to her recognition by associates as the belle of every occasion. The "belle complex," which was a dominant force in her life, seems to explain her unwillingness after the war to settle down with her husband in the seclusion of a plantation cabin.

In addition to being vain and proud she was selfish and self-centered. She evidenced no concern for humanitarianism or philanthropy. There is no record of her making clothing for needy Confederate soldiers or helping provide relief for indigent families. She rarely went to a hospital, and when she did it was as a casual visitor rather than as a minister to the suffering. During the war, despite the fact that she was a refugee much of the time, she lived a comfortable, sheltered life with well-fixed relatives and friends. When her husband went to Canada and had an opportunity to send or bring commodities through the blockade, Virginia's repeated requests were not for medicines to relieve the suffering but for finery with which to adorn herself.

Still another weakness was her lack of intellectual depth. Her reading seems to have been limited largely to newspapers and fashion magazines. In the long list of items that she requested from Canada in November 1864, the only reading material that she included was "some books of fashion, Sept., Oct., and Nov. numbers." She was deeply interested in politics and seems to have been well-informed about political issues and leaders. But social affairs were her dominant concern and she showed no inclination to delve into philosophical matters or to probe life's profundities. She read the Bible and enjoyed a good sermon, but if she seriously analyzed the religious instruction to which she was exposed or attempted to apply it to social problems of the time, she left no record of the fact. Her writings offer no indication that she experienced any feeling of guilt about slavery such as that manifested by Mrs. Chesnut in her *Diary from Dixie*.

But Virginia had her good points. She was a sparkling, attractive person, whose company was enjoyed by both men and women. She had a quick mind, a keen sense of humor, enormous vitality, and an exceptional gift for mimicry. She was gregarious, fun-loving, a lively conversationalist, and a graceful dancer. She played the piano well enough to provide accompaniment for party singing, and her letters indicate that she had more than ordinary talent for writing. Apparently, she was not beautiful and her increase in weight from 117 in 1852 to 155 in 1863 must have put a considerable strain on both her wardrobe and her appearance. But the eagerness with which men sought her attention, from her girlhood to her old age, affords convincing evidence of her abundant charm. Mrs. Chesnut in her diary quotes a Richmond doctor as saying in a comment about the Confederacy's leading ladies: "Mrs. Clay . . . I proclaim her supreme for wits and beauty as well as refinement."[68] Mrs. Roger A. Pryor, reminiscing forty years after the war about social life in Washington in the 1850s stated: "But the wittiest and brightest of them all was Mrs. Clay. . . . She was extremely clever, the soul of every company."[69]

Virginia was forthright and courageous in stating her views and upholding her convictions. This quality was vividly demonstrated in her confrontations with Secretary Stanton and President Johnson for the release of her husband. In one exchange with Johnson she asked him who was President, he or Stanton; and on another occasion, she told him that he should get rid of the cabinet inherited from Lincoln and surround himself with one reflecting his own views. At first the Tennessee plebeian and the Alabama aristocrat regarded each other with suspicion and dislike, but in the course of their candid confrontations they developed mutual respect and goodwill.

Virginia demonstrated exceptional will power and persistence in the long, arduous campaign for her husband's parole. Although she was sometimes reduced to tears by the frustrations and set-backs she experienced, she never despaired. To her perseverance must go much of the credit for Clement Clay's parole more than a year before Jefferson Davis's release.

It is only fair to note that, despite Virginia's excessive concern with herself, there were times when she manifested deep sympathy and great kindness toward others. Her earnest solicitude for her husband during his absence in Canada and his imprisonment at Fort Monroe has already been mentioned. With her strong affection for children she experienced profound grief when both Celeste Clay and Loula Hammond lost their infants during the war and she did all she could to solace the bereaved mothers. She also devoted considerable time and effort to the comfort and care of her aged, ailing parents-in-law during the early months of her husband's imprisonment.

Finally, cognizance should be taken of Virginia's strength in adversity. When the Civil War and Reconstruction deprived her of affluence, position, and all the things to which she attached so much importance, she did not succumb to bitterness and sink into despair. It is true, to her discredit, that too often and too long she forsook her husband for the bright lights and gay associations of the city. But she endured, and in so doing, she demonstrated a ruggedness of mind and body that distinguish her as "a strong woman."

3

Varina Howell Davis—
First Lady,
Wife, and Mother

Varina Davis recalled in 1890 that her husband's countenance reflected profound grief when, on February 10, 1861, in their Mississippi garden at Brierfield he read the telegram informing him of his election to the presidency of the newly formed Southern Confederacy. She failed to give her own reaction to the message, but it must have been unfavorable. She knew that her husband ''neither desired nor expected the position''; moreover, her years as a statesman's wife in Washington had brought her as much pain as pleasure. Still, she respected the sense of responsibility that impelled her husband to accept the high position thrust upon him and dutifully joined him in preparations for the move to Montgomery. He left Brierfield the next day while she remained at home to complete arrangements for a long absence. Not until early March was she able to join her spouse at the Confederate capital.

The woman who thus reluctantly became the Confederacy's one and only First Lady was well qualified for the position. Born near

Natchez on May 7, 1826, and christened Varina Anne Banks Howell, she was of distinguished heritage. Her paternal grandfather, Richard Howell, a Revolutionary veteran of Welsh descent, was governor of New Jersey from 1793 to 1801. The governor's third son, William Burr Howell, after service as a Marine officer in the War of 1812, migrated to Natchez, where in 1823 he married Margaret Louisa Kempe, daughter of Colonel James Kempe, a cultured Irishman, and Margaret Graham Kempe, a Virginian. Colonel Kempe owned several plantations and was one of the recognized leaders of the Natchez area.

Varina was the second child and the first daughter of William and Margaret Howell, both respected members of their community. Although her father was a poor manager, he was able to rear Varina in privileged circumstances. When she was ten years old she enrolled in Madame Grelaud's school in Philadephia where she remained for two terms. Nothing is known of this institution or its curriculum. But an aunt who resided in Philadelphia, and who helped look after the child, wrote Varina's mother shortly after her matriculation that she was adjusting well to her new environment and that "Mrs. Grelaud says she is very smart & capable and improves fast."[1]

The best of Varina's education was obtained informally from a bachelor friend, Judge George Winchester, a native of Massachusetts and a graduate of Harvard who lived in the Howell home, The Briers, and who tutored Varina for twelve years. A deep bond of affection developed between teacher and pupil. In 1850, Varina, then a senator's wife, wrote her mother: "Kiss the dear old Judgy for me and tell him that I feel every day the older I grow and the more I see of the world what a good friend he has always been to me and mine." Many years later, when writing a memoir of her husband, she referred to Judge Winchester as "a saintly man to whom I owe the little learning I have acquired, and also the realization of my childish ideal of 'Great-heart'." She added that he was a hard teacher, but that "the most valuable lessons I learned were not from the Latin or English classics . . . but from the pure high standard of right, of which his course was the exemplar.'' Judge Winchester was a Whig, as was Varina's father and most of the Natchez uppercrust; the tutor passed on to his pupil the political views contained in the *National Intelligencer*, which, according to Varina, "everybody took."[2]

While Varina was rounding out her education under Judge Winchester's capable and affectionate guidance, Joseph Emory Davis, one of her father's oldest and best friends, was becoming increasingly concerned about the welfare and happiness of his much younger brother, Jefferson. Reputedly a millionaire, Joseph owned a very large tract of land on the Mississippi River about thirty miles below Vicksburg. He had been instrumental in obtaining an appointment for Jefferson at West Point and had followed with pride his brother's seven-year career as an officer in the regular army. When Jefferson resigned his commission in 1835 and married Knox Taylor, daughter of his former commanding officer, Colonel Zachary Taylor, Joe gave the newlyweds a plantation, Brierfield, adjoining his own, The Hurricane.

Within three months of marriage, Knox died of fever. The disconsolate young widower retired to Brierfield, and began a life of seclusion, devoted mainly to clearing additional land, building a dwelling, and directing the labor of his fifteen slaves. In a few years he established himself as a successful cotton planter. His principal recreation was reading in his brother's excellent library.

Joe enjoyed Jefferson's companionship, but he knew that the perpetuation of his brother's self-imposed isolation would preclude a full realization of his exceptional potential. It was probably with a view of bringing Jefferson out of the doldrums that Joseph in 1843, eight years after Knox's death, persuaded William and Margaret Howell to let their seventeen-year-old daughter, Varina, visit The Hurricane during the Christmas holidays. Shortly after meeting Jefferson Davis, Varina wrote her mother about her first impressions of the thirty-six-year-old widower:

I do not know whether this Mr. Jefferson Davis is young or old. He looks both at times. . . . He impresses me as a remarkable kind of man, but of uncertain temper, and has a way of taking for granted that everybody agrees with him when he expresses an opinion, which offends me; yet he is most agreeable and has a peculiarly sweet voice and a winning manner of asserting himself. The fact is, he is the kind of person I should expect to rescue one from a mad dog at any risk, but to insist upon a stoical indifference to the fright afterward. I do not think I shall ever like him as I do his brother Joe. Would you believe it, he is refined and cultivated, and yet he is a Democrat![3]

During the days that followed, Varina and Jefferson frequently slipped away from the Davis kin who had assembled at The Hurricane for a Christmas house party. They read, talked, walked, and took long horseback rides. Both were accomplished riders and it was probably this activity that Varina enjoyed most.

During these pleasant associations, romance quickly developed and before Varina left The Hurricane early in February 1844 she and Jefferson became engaged. Thereafter love letters occasionally passed between them. Those written by Varina apparently were lost or destroyed, but some of Jefferson's communications were preserved by descendants. Jefferson's letters, usually opening with such salutations as "My own dearest Varina," or "My dearest, my own one," show that a man known in public life as "aloof and austere" was in relationships with intimates capable of the greatest tenderness and solicitude.[4] Varina's mother at first disapproved of Davis as a prospective son-in-law, probably because of his age. But Davis's visit to Natchez in the spring of 1844, together with strong endorsements from Judge Winchester and Margaret Howell's mother, overcame parental opposition to the betrothal. Shortly afterward, Davis became actively involved in the presidential campaign which resulted in the election of James

K. Polk, and Varina experienced a prolonged siege of ill health. Correspondence became irregular, some of it reflecting a decided cooling of romantic ardor. But early in 1845 relations took a turn for the better and on February 26, 1845, Varina and Jefferson were married in a simple home ceremony. On their honeymoon they visited Jefferson's sister, Mrs. Luther L. Smith, at Locust Grove, Louisiana, and called on Jefferson's eighty-five-year-old mother, Jane, at Woodville, Mississippi. The old lady was unable to rise from her chair, but Varina found her "still fair to look on," with her eyes shining "and her complexion clear and white as a child's."[5] The couple completed their honeymoon with a six-weeks sojourn at the St. Charles Hotel in New Orleans.

The house to which Jefferson took his bride at Brierfield was rough but spacious. This was to be their home until it was replaced by a more pretentious dwelling five years later. Varina adapted herself well to the new environment, and she and her husband spent many happy hours together reading, riding horseback, conversing, and beautifying the premises. The bride found special pleasure in tending the flowers and shrubs that grew in abundance about the house. Her letters to her mother indicate that she was a happy, industrious wife, thoroughly devoted to her Jeff. The awe with which she regarded him at first gradually gave way to an easy companionship marked by mutual affection and trust. Two months after the marriage Jefferson wrote his mother-in-law: "I think she grows calmer, discreeter, happier & lovelier with each passing day"; and Davis was not at all inclined to exaggeration.[6]

The greatest potential threat to serenity at Brierfield was the near-presence and overprotectiveness of Brother Joe. In 1847 the two families quarreled over Joe's proposal that Jeff share Brierfield with a widowed sister and her children then residing with Joe. Varina vetoed the suggestion. This difference healed with the passing of time, as did many others, but beneath the surface of politeness there lingered latent tensions which produced chronic uneasiness in both households.

In the autumn of 1845 Jefferson was elected to the House of Representatives. Before departing for Washington he made an address welcoming John C. Calhoun to Vicksburg. Varina was tremendously impressed by the eloquence of her husband and that of the distinguished visitor. She conversed afterward with Calhoun and was delighted that he treated her as an "intellectual equal." At a ball which concluded the day's activities she was shocked by the dress and demeanor of Mrs.William Gwin, whose husband in 1850 was to become senator from California. "Mrs. Gwin," Varina wrote naively to her mother, "was dressed in a black velvet cut so low in the neck that it was absolutely indecent, no sleeves to her dress, neck and arms perfectly bare, every movement of her body exposing more of her person than I should have thought any *lady* would care about, so much of it indeed that I could not look at her without blushing and feeling ashamed."[7]

When Jeff and Varina went to Washington for the opening of Congress in December 1845, they moved into a boarding house on Pennsylvania Avenue and shared a mess with other members of the Mississippi delegation. On January 30, 1846, she wrote her mother: "Jeff . . . has not been well since we arrived here he sits up until two or three o'clock at night writing—until his eyes even lose their beauty to *me*, they look so red and painful." Varina adapted herself to the simple way of life that accorded with her husband's inclinations and habits. She gave informal dances occasionally, went sightseeing, listened to congressional speeches, and attended functions given by the President and other notables. Her reaction to most of the dignitaries seems to have been favorable, but after attending a White House dinner in January 1846 she wrote her mother: "Mrs. P[olk] came up dressed to death. She is a very handsome woman . . . [but] talks too much a la President's wife—is to[o] anxious to please. Polk is an insignificant looking little man." She described as "most delightful" an evening during which she, Charles Ingersoll, and George M. Dallas talked of Byron, Wordsworth, Dante, and Virgil. She matured rapidly in the stimulating atmosphere of Washington. On April 3, 1846 she wrote her mother: "My manners are much improved. . . . I have lost a great deal of that embarrassed, angry looking manner which made me [show] to so much disadvantage."[8]

Outbreak of war between the United States and Mexico in May 1846 brought the first major crisis in Varina's married life. Against her strong opposition Jefferson accepted the colonelcy of a Mississippi regiment. On June 6, Varina wrote her mother: "I have cried until I am stupid. . . . If Jeff was a cross, bad husband, old, ugly or stupid, I could better bear for him to go . . . but he is so tender and good that I feel like he ought never to leave me. . . . I might quarrel a month and he would not get mad."[9]

Jefferson gave Varina the choice of residing in Washington or in Mississippi during his Mexican service. She elected to stay at The Hurricane so that she might consult frequently with James Pemberton, the trusted Negro who had long served her husband as personal aide and overseer, concerning affairs at Brierfield. In August she received a letter from Jefferson telling of his safe arrival at the Rio Grande, assuring her that he had remembered her request on the subject of profanity and had improved; he advised her to be pious, calm, useful, charitable, and temperate. As Jefferson had feared, Varina became very unhappy at The Hurricane. Joe found fault with her management of Brierfield, and his wife and sisters were offended by her offishness and hauteur. When Varina discovered that Joe had drawn a will for Jefferson before the latter's departure, bequeathing a share of Jefferson's estate to his two widowed sisters, she went home to her parents. There she became so ill of mind and body that she wrote her husband a letter impelling him at great inconvenience to obtain leave and pay her a visit. They met at Brierfield early in November for two weeks, during which Jefferson was able to bring some relief to her troubled spirit.

Early in March 1847 she received a letter from Jefferson telling her that he had been in battle at Buena Vista and had received a wound in the foot which he described as "painful but . . . by no means dangerous."[10] From other sources she learned that the valor and resourcefulness of her husband, who at a critical point in the action arranged his men in a V-formation to repel a formidable Mexican charge, was a key factor in saving the day for General Zachary Taylor.

In June, Colonel Davis came home a great hero and resumed life as a planter at Brierfield. He had to use crutches for two years and the wound caused considerable pain for a long time afterward. In the summer of 1847 Varina, basking in the praise heaped on her wounded spouse, wrote her mother: "Jeff's heel is better, . . . he lets me dress it, which you know is a great pleasure to me."[11]

Two months after his return home, Davis was appointed to a vacancy in the United States Senate. Varina, plagued by illness, stayed in Mississippi during her husband's first months in Washington. On January 24, 1849, she wrote him from Natchez: "If you have no fear for yourself, have it for your Winnie, your thoughtless, dependent wife, and guard your health as you would my life. Sweetest, best husband, don't go out at night, don't drink wine, don't eat any fruit." Davis was undoubtedly pleased by his twenty-two-year-old wife's pledges of devotion, but the dignified senator must have blushed when, at the end of her letter of January 24, 1849, he read the words: "My own bright love, farewell. Kiss wife, and say goodnight. Winnie is Husband's baby and baby is your devoted wife, Winnie Davis."[12]

Varina was with her husband when the Thirty-second Congress opened in December 1849. Their apartment adjoined the United States Hotel, where they took their meals in a "mess" which included several other congressmen. Of this group the towering, jovial Senator Robert Toombs of Georgia was the most versatile and the most gregarious, but in her memoir Varina states that he and her husband were never congenial because their habits and manners were so different. Davis served on the committee on military affairs, entered actively into major debates, and early in his senatorial career won recognition as one of the most effective speakers in Congress. Concerning this period of her husband's career, Varina wrote shortly after his death: "Very little of Mr. Davis's time was devoted to the claims of society. He was so impervious to the influence of anything but principle in shaping his political course that he underrated the effect of social intercourse in determining the action of public men and never sought to exert it in behalf of his own policy. In consequence we went out but little. . . . In rare cases, where he was attached to the friends who gave the invitation, he accepted."[13]

Among invitations accepted were those issued by President and Mrs. Zachary Taylor, with whom the Davises were on good terms. Following the Taylors' New Year's reception of 1850, Varina wrote her mother that she did not enjoy it, but after dining at the White House the following May she reported "a sweet time. . . . the only dinner party I have enjoyed for a long time."[14] Both the Davises were at Taylor's bedside when the President died on July 9, 1850, and they did what they could to comfort his bereaved wife and daughters.

In the debates over the Compromise of 1850 and all other measures involving slavery, Davis strongly defended the South's "peculiar institution" and the right of slave owners to take their Negro property into any Federal territory. Then, as later, he believed in the right of secession but thought that the right should be exercised only as a last resort. Varina was in full accord with these views. Once, in 1849, she told him that she thought his reply to Senator John Hale's attack on slavery was a "little too violent."[15] But such criticism was exceptional.

On September 3, 1851, Davis resigned from the Senate to become a Democratic candidate for governor in place of John A. Quitman, who was running a poor race against the Unionist contestant, Henry S. Foote. Despite the handicap of an illness which led to severe inflammation of his left eye, Davis improved Democratic prospects; still, he lost to Foote by 999 votes. The defeat was much less of a disappointment to Varina than to her husband. She wrote her mother afterward: "You know my heart never went with Jeff in politics or soldiering." She settled down happily in the new house that had just been completed at Brierfield, devoting herself to gardening, making clothes for her younger brothers and sisters, and other domestic activities. Unprecedented joy came to Brierfield on July 30, 1852, when Varina gave birth to a son, who was named Samuel Emerson. Tragically, the greatly adored child died shortly before his second birthday.

Davis campaigned vigorously for Franklin Pierce in 1852 and a few weeks after the election the victorious Pierce asked his Mississippi friend to become secretary of war. This request provoked another crisis at Brierfield. Varina, supremely happy in her plantation home and acutely aware that her spouse was in better health and spirit than at any previous time in their marriage, strongly opposed a return to Washington. At first Davis seemed inclined to respect her wishes, but eventually he yielded to the President's persuasions and was sworn in as secretary of war on March 7, 1853.

Varina, always a dutiful wife until the postwar years, swallowed her disappointment and after allowing Jefferson sufficient time to rent a house large enough to accommodate her, her younger brother and sister, her baby, and a nurse, headed for the capital. Except for the death of their child, the next four years proved far happier than she had anticipated. Her husband greatly enjoyed his cabinet position and achieved outstanding success and recognition. Largely as a result of this satisfaction he enjoyed good health. He and Varina were close friends of the Pierces. They entertained more than previously and their guests included the ranking members of the governmental and diplomatic circles as well as leading intellectuals of the capital, such as Alexander Bache, Louis Agassiz, and Joseph Henry. Varina charmed visitors with her poise and sprightliness, while her husband impressed them favorably with his dignity, intelligence, and superior gifts as a raconteur.

Varina's mother formed a very favorable impression of the society in which the Davises moved when she visited Washington in the autumn of 1854. She noted with special approval that the people whom she met were well-informed and articulate, and that they attached more importance to intellect and talent than to material possessions.[16]

The heartbreak resulting from little Sam's death in 1854 was eased by the birth on February 25, 1855, of Margaret Howell, named for Varina's mother and sister. "Polly," as the baby was called, soon established herself firmly in the affection of her parents. On January 16, 1857, Varina gave birth to a son, Jefferson, Jr., but postnatal complications kept Varina in bed for more than two weeks and impaired her health for several months. On January 31 she wrote her mother: "I am not dead, though I have been very near it. . . . The baby is a very fine one. He looks exactly like his Father. . . . He has a look of Pa in his eyes."[17]

On March 5, 1857, the day after completing his term as secretary of war, Davis reentered the United States Senate, then in special session. In May he took his family to Brierfield. After a brief stay there Varina and the children went to Mississippi City on the Gulf Coast where they spent the remainder of the summer, while Jefferson divided his time between looking after the plantation and making political speeches. When late in the fall the family returned to Washington in anticipation of the opening of Congress, they took along Varina's sister Maggie, now in her teens, and her brother Jeffy D., who was ten, and put them in school. Helping out the Howells was a practice to which Jefferson became accustomed soon after marrying into the family, but he seemed genuinely fond of his wife's people and he never complained about sharing responsibility for their support. In January 1854, Varina wrote her mother: "Dont make yourself wretched about paying for Maggie's education for Jeff is in heart and in truth your son and would serve you to the last and is devoted to Maggie."[18] In effect, Maggie and

Jeffy D. became full-fledged members of the Davis household.

Back in Washington Varina entered a round of social activities which made heavy demands on her relatively limited wardrobe as well as her physical stamina. On December 16, 1857, she wrote her mother: "The lancers, a new dance, is all the rage, and all the old married women [she was now thirty] lance but me. Of all things it is the solemnest performance, being nothing more nor less than a very involute cotillion and the dancers look so solemn and at a loss it is funny."[19] She did not go as often to the White House as she did during the Taylor and Pierce administrations, but she was on good terms with Harriet Lane, Buchanan's niece and hostess, and was impressed by her poise and charm. At the famous costume ball given by Senator and Mrs. William Gwin in April 1858, she played the part of Madame de Staël and won the high praise of her companions. While she continued to be recognized as one of the leading figures in capital society as long as she remained a part of it, she found greater satisfaction in effectively fulfilling her role as wife and mother.

As a senator's wife, she followed closely the political discussions of the time. A principal issue early in 1858 was the Kansas question. Davis fought earnestly for admission of the state with the proslavery Lecompton Constitution, but the bill was defeated in the House. Largely because of the strain engendered by this struggle, Davis's health broke down in February and he suffered a long and painful siege of neuralgia and glaucoma which threatened to make him totally blind. (At this time, if not earlier, according to a study published by Dr. W. A. Evans in 1942, he lost vision in his left eye).[20]

In June 1858 Davis and his family went to New England for the complete rest ordered by his doctor. In Maine they enjoyed picnics, clam bakes, and camping trips. They spent some time in Boston where Varina listened with pride as her husband spoke to an appreciative audience at Faneuil Hall. The invigorating atmosphere, the cordiality of the people, the leisurely reading, and the stimulating talk made the trip a memorable experience for Varina and restored the health of her ailing husband. At the end of the vacation, Jefferson went to Mississippi to mend his political fences and to check on affairs at Brierfield. In March 1859 he had to make another trip south to salvage what he could from a destructive flood which inundated the plantation. During these absences, Varina spent much time with her good friends, among whom was Mrs. Joseph E. Johnston, who later was to be one of her bitterest enemies. Varina also found much pleasure in attending her children and reporting their sayings and doings to her parents and her absent husband. Both children were precocious. Polly, then four, would stand by the yard gate until she could get a passing pedestrian to release the latch which was beyond her reach, and take off to a neighbor's house for an unauthorized visit. Little Jeff, who was only two, would threaten to strike his mother when she slapped him and would vociferously proclaim superior devotion to his father. [21]

On April 18, 1859, while Jefferson was still in Mississippi, Varina bore him another son. The day before the baby's arrival, she wrote "Dear Banny" (a nickname of uncertain origin which she lately had given her husband) that she had just completed franking two hundred envelopes and that the feeling of doing something for him brought her special happiness. She was obviously uneasy about her approaching confinement, but there was no plea stated or implied for Jefferson to hurry home. She had come a long way since she summoned him from the Mexican front, and she indicated realization of the fact. "Often since you have been away this time," she stated, "I have experienced that queer annihilation of responsibility and of time and gone back fourteen long years to the anxious loving girl, so little of use, yet so devoted to you."[22] Time, children, affliction, and the joys and cares of daily association had forged a strong bond of affection between the fifty-year-old senator and his thirty-two-year-old wife.

This is not to say that their marriage had reached a state of complete bliss. Soon after the fourth baby's birth, a disagreement arose concerning his name. Varina had her heart set on calling him William, for her father. But Jefferson wished to recognize his brother Joe—and so the infant was christened Joseph Evan Davis. Varina poured out her resentment to her mother in a letter admitting her husband's right to name their son, but objecting strongly to thus honoring a person from whom she had suffered so much unkindness. But the surge of anger quickly subsided, and Varina was soon writing Jefferson that "all the sweetness of our happiest hours seems to have returned with his birth."[23]

As a result of the alarm and passion aroused by John Brown's Raid of October 16, 1859, feelings were very tense when the Thirty-sixth Congress assembled in December. In the Senate as in the House, the most acrimonious debate was focused on the question of slavery in the territories. Davis was a leading supporter of the extreme Southern position that the Constitution required Congress to protect slavery in all Federal territories. This brought him into sharp conflict with Stephen A. Douglas, who advocated letting settlers decide for themselves whether the territories should be slave or free, and with Republicans such as William H. Seward, who thought that the power of the national government should be used to prevent the expansion of slavery.

Varina and other congressional wives often sat in the galleries to give moral support to their husbands; the increasing emotional involvement of the women helped intensify the antagonisms of their menfolk. The growing discord in politics enhanced the strain of social relationships and made entertaining a difficult and delicate undertaking.

As early as September 1856, Varina had denounced Senator Douglas, then about to marry Adele Cutts, as "a dirty speculator and party trickster," a broken-down drunkard who was using his first wife's money to buy "an elegant, well-bred woman" from a poor and proud father.[24] Her loathing for him increased as he became her husband's leading antagonist in the Senate debate over slavery. On him she placed major blame for the split in the Democratic party. She heartily seconded her husband's support of John Breckinridge's Southern rights group in the presidential campaign of 1860. She did not know Abraham Lincoln, but she shared fully her husband's view that the Republican party was hostile to slavery and that Lincoln's election would spell the end of Southern security within the Union.

Admiral David Porter, in March 1865, told Secretary of the Navy Gideon Welles that he had talked with Varina on the night that she heard of South Carolina's secession and that she was highly elated by the news. [25] While Porter's recollection may have been accurate, it seems more reasonable to conclude that Varina, like her husband, regarded secession with mixed emotions when it actually came; certainly that was the way she recalled her sentiments when preparing her memoir in the 1880s. She wrote then that neither she nor Davis slept the night before he gave his valedictory in the Senate on January 21, 1861. She sat in the audience as he spoke and her report of what he said reflects more sadness than joy. "Not his wife alone but all who sat spellbound before him," she wrote, "knew how genuine was his grief and entered into the spirit of his loving appeal. . . . Inexpressibly sad he left the chamber, with but faint hope; and that night I heard the oft reiterated prayer, 'May God have us in his holy keeping, and grant that before it is too late peaceful councils may prevail.' "[26]

Davis wrote Franklin Pierce a letter the next day indicating that he had little hope of peace. "Civil War has only horror for me," he stated, "but whatever circumstances demand shall be met as a duty and I trust be so discharged that you will not be ashamed of our former connection or cease to be my friend."[27] This was his mood when three weeks later he answered the summons to become Chief Executive of the Confederate States of America.

According to Varina's memoir, the prospect of war weighed heavily on her mind as she journeyed by boat down the Mississippi and up the Alabama to join her husband late in February 1861. But her spirits were lifted by the enthusiastic reception accorded her as she rode through Montgomery to temporary quarters at the Exchange Hotel. Her morale received another boost when a few weeks later she moved with her family into the two-story dwelling that was the Confederacy's first White House.[28] The famous English journalist, William H. Russell, wrote after attending one of Mrs. Davis's receptions early in May 1861: "The modest villa in which the President lives is painted white . . . and stands in a small garden. The door was open. A colored servant took in our names and Mr. Browne presented me to Mrs. Davis. . . . There was no affectation of state or ceremony in the reception. Mrs. Davis, whom some of her friends call 'Queen Varina,' is a comely, sprightly woman, verging on matronhood, of good figure and manners, well-dressed, ladylike and clever, and she seemed a great favorite with those around her."[29] The appellation, "Queen Varina," which was to follow the First Lady to Richmond, did not always connote the friendliness that Russell implied. From the beginning some who observed Varina in her new role thought she was inclined to put on regal airs, but their views may have been based largely on envy. Her years as a leader in Washington society had given her an experience and confidence that enabled her to move with ease among all classes of people. Adding much to her appeal as hostess was the attractiveness of her household which included her sister Maggie, a sparkling, handsome girl; Varina's own Margaret who at six was smart, venturesome, and beautiful; and four-year-old Jeff and two-year-old Joe, lively, intelligent boys who charmed all who knew them, especially their parents. In general, the people of Montgomery warmed to the Davises and the First Family responded in kind. Jefferson was bedeviled by officeseekers, not all of whom could be satisfied, and concern over the enormous problems of setting up a new government weighed heavily on his spirit, frazzled his nerves, and aggravated his chronic insomnia. But he kept himself under strict control, was uniformly courteous to visitors, and consistently kindly and affectionate toward his family.

The outbreak of war in mid-April stepped up the tempo of life in Montgomery, bringing in hordes of people and heaping new burdens on the President. Unfortunately, the Chief Executive tried personally to look after many details that ought to have been delegated to subordinates. As a result, he suffered more and more from nervous fatigue and Varina grew increasingly anxious about his well-being. But she kept up her weekly receptions and presented a calm front to all comers. Congestion, heat, and scarcity of food, however, made life increasingly uncomfortable. Varina was glad when the decision was made in May to move the capital to Richmond. Even so, in the perspective of time, she would look back on her weeks in Montgomery as the most agreeable part of her Confederate career.

The President traveled to Richmond late in May; Varina with the children made the trip a few days later. After a long, hard journey, Varina was pleased to be met at the railroad station by her husband with a carriage and four horses provided by the city. "As we proceeded up the street," she wrote her mother, "bouquets were showered into the carriage and hurrahs for the children. It is perfect man worship. The place one vast camp."[30] The family lived for about a month in an apartment at the Spotswood Hotel where at first, according to Varina, everything was topsy-turvy and she had not a moment to herself. In August Davis moved to the Brockenbrough mansion, a three-story brick dwelling completed in 1818, which was to serve as the Confederate White House for the remainder of the war. The house was located on a high hill near the customs building in which the President's office was located. Behind the White House was a large garden which gave Varina a sense of "feeling at home."

At first the ladies of Virginia's aristocratic old families were reserved in their relationships with the Confederacy's First Lady. Their manner suggested to Varina the wariness with which the

British greeted strangers. She continued the democratic usages that she had followed in Montgomery, with fortnightly levees open to all and smaller gatherings in between for special guests or intimate friends. On August 10, 1861, Mrs. Joseph Davis, who with her husband and family were house guests of the President, wrote her niece that Varina was receiving guests and that her parlors sometimes teemed with strangers. In time Varina developed warmer relationships with many of the established families, some of whom she already knew from Washington associations. R.F.W. Allston, a prominent South Carolinian who called on the Davises in mid-July 1861, wrote his wife: ''The president . . . looks very feeble. . . . Mrs. Davis has not lost any flesh since you saw her and is as animated as ever. She moves about, receives and talks, as in a triumph, and is strong in having her country women about her as a sort of court.''[31]

The great popularity enjoyed by the Davises in the early months of the war began to wane in the summer and fall of 1861. This was in part the result of war weariness and the failure of the South to win its independence quickly, as ''fire-eating'' secessionists had promised. But the development of personal antagonisms was also a contributing factor and in this Varina was unavoidably involved.

In August 1861, Davis rated the generals, supposedly in accordance with a Confederate law which stated that officers who came into Confederate service from the Federal army should have the same relative rank that they had in the old organization. Joseph E. Johnston expected to outrank all other officers appointed because he was the only one who rated as high as brigadier general at the time of quitting Federal service. But Davis, in disregard of the law, ranked Samuel Cooper, Albert S. Johnston, and Robert E. Lee above Joseph E. Johnston. Davis in 1878 justified his action on the ground that Johnston owed his high Federal ranking to the fact that he was quartermaster general, a staff position, and that he did not think staff ranking should be considered in determining relative rank in Confederate service. But Davis did not apply this formula in rating Samuel Cooper first among the Confederate generals, because Cooper was only a colonel in the Federal army and he held that rank by virtue of his staff position of adjutant general. Johnston's response to Davis's action was a long and angry letter in which he stated, "It transfers me from the position of first rank to that of fourth. . . . This is a blow aimed at me only." On September 14 the President curtly replied: "Your letter of the 12th instant is . . . utterly one-sided, and its insinuations as unfounded as they are unbecoming."[32]

Meanwhile, relationships between Johnston's wife, Lydia, and Varina had been declining from the closeness of prior times. After the quarrel over Johnston's rank, they deteriorated rapidly and Lydia became permanently embittered toward the Davises. Before the quarrel she had referred to Varina as a "western belle"; afterward the designation became "western woman."[33]

Joseph and Lydia Johnston had many influential friends, among them Senator Louis Wigfall of Texas and his wife Charlotte. In the early months of the war, the Wigfalls and the Davises were friendly but after the Johnstons turned against the President and his wife, enmity developed between the Wigfalls and the Davises. Charlotte depicted Varina as "a coarse western woman" and Wigfall became the leader of an anti-Davis bloc in the Senate.[34] Mrs. Chesnut was of the opinion that Wigfall and Davis could have remained friends had it not been for the falling out of their wives. Mrs. Chesnut may have been right, for she was a very perceptive lady.

The President was very quick to resent any criticism of his wife. Some governmental officials attributed Davis's failure to promote Confederate Quartermaster General A. C. Myers from colonel to general in 1863, as Congress desired, to a grudge growing out of Mrs. Myers' reference to Varina as an old squaw.[35] The degree of Davis's sensitiveness in matters relating to his wife is brought out in his angry protest when he heard that Dr. Alexander Garnett, his physician, had written General John A. Wise (Garnett's father-in-law), that Varina had sent Wise her love in appreciation of a small gift she had recently received from the general. Wise was so disgusted by the President's taking offense at an innocuous bit of humor that he wrote Garnett: "There is a screw loose in him. . . . He is a small, weak, little, jaundiced bigot and vain pretender."[36]

Varina apparently paid little attention to criticism directed at her, but she deeply resented denunciations of her husband. In August 1861, Mary Chesnut noted in her diary: "Mrs. Davis is being utterly upset. She is beginning to hear the carping and fault-finding to which the President is subjected."[37] It is doubtful that few besides Mrs. Chesnut knew that Varina was disturbed by criticism directed at the President.

The birth of William Howell Davis on December 16, 1861, caused a temporary suspension of public levees, but these were resumed early the next year. Varina braved a heavy rain on February 22 to attend her husband's inauguration as President under the permanent Constitution and presided over the White House reception which was held that night. Diarist J. B. Jones stated that continuing rain made the occasion lugubrious, but added that "Mrs. Davis seemed in spirits."[38] Congressman J. R. McLean of North Carolina wrote his wife the following day: "I was introduced to President Davis and Mrs. Davis. He was dressed in a plain black suit, and is a gentleman of elegant manners and was perfectly at ease. . . . His wife is large and somewhat fleshy—not handsome but rather good looking & agreeable, but I thought not the equal of the President. His little son and daughter, beautiful and intelligent children, stood near them in the reception room."[39] Varina may have been having a slight weight problem following William's birth, but she was five feet and ten inches tall and a photograph taken about this time shows her to be pleasingly plump rather than fat.

Military reverses of early 1862 intensified antagonism to the President. By March there was talk in Congress of removing him from office.[40] Writing of this period, in her memoir Varina stated that opposition to the administration "might have been weakened by daily social intercourse, and habituated as we were to giving numerous entertainments of an official character, we should gladly have kept up the custom." But the President, whom she characterized as "a nervous dyspeptic by habit," so "abnormally sensitive to disapprobation [that] even a child's disapproval discomposed him," was so distressed by the mounting criticisms that he ordered a curtailment of entertainments. As Varina put it: "He said he could do either one duty or the other—give entertainments or administer the Government—and he fancied he was expected to perform the latter service in preference; and so we ceased to entertain except at formal receptions or informal breakfasts given to as many as Mr. Davis's health permitted us to invite. In the evening he was too exhausted to receive formal visitors." This restriction on entertainment continued through most of the war. Varina was keenly aware of the injury done to the presidential image and influence, but she accepted it as an inevitable consequence of her husband's high-strung temperament and heavy responsibilities.[41]

As the Federals approached Richmond in May 1862, Davis sent Varina and the children to Raleigh, North Carolina, where she remained until late August. Shortly before she left, Davis, who was reared a Baptist but had no church affiliation, became a communicant of St. Paul's Episcopal Church. He was now criticized by the Richmond *Examiner* for counting his beads when he should be repelling the Federals and for sending his family to safety while ordinary folk risked the dangers of invasion. Varina was bitterly criticized for fleeing the capital in time of danger. Catherine Edmonston, a North Carolina woman, wrote in her diary on May 13, 1862: "Mrs. Davis has left Richmond and gone to Raleigh, fairly deserted her colors. I fear she is not a woman of the true stamp. I fear she does not strengthen her husband, or she would never have abandoned her post & set such an example to the rest of the women of the Confederacy." On May 20 she wrote:

"Mrs. Davis is, I hear, a Philadelphia woman! That accounts for
. . . her flight from Richmond."[42]

Hardly had Varina reached Raleigh when she confronted an
unforeseen peril in the serious illness of her infant, Billy. The baby
recovered but only after a near brush with death. During the weeks
of separation, the President kept his wife fully informed concerning military operations. Among items of news that he passed on to
her was the pillaging of Brierfield by Federal raiders and the flight
of Joe Davis and his family from their Hurricane residence, which
was then burned. Varina's parents, who had barely escaped from
New Orleans when General Benjamin F. Butler's forces occupied
that city in May, were living in Montgomery; there her father
obtained employment in the commissary department.

Varina returned to Richmond in time to help celebrate the
Confederate victory at Second Manassas on August 30, 1862.
Lee's repulse at Sharpsburg in September and Bragg's setback in
Kentucky in October were disappointing, but at year's end the
military picture was brightened by the defeat of Burnside at
Fredericksburg and Sherman at Vicksburg. A source of personal
pleasure to Varina was the return to Richmond of Mary Chesnut,
whose husband became the President's aide in October. With
Varina's help the Chesnuts found living quarters in Mrs. Lyon's
residence, only two blocks from the White House. Varina and
Mary, kindred spirits, spent many enjoyable hours conversing,
shopping, exchanging visits, and going to parties. Neither entered
actively into hospital work, Mary because the sight of blood made
her faint and Varina because, as she wrote in her memoir, "Mr.
Davis felt it best for me not to expose the men to the restraint my
presence might have imposed." But Varina occasionally visited
hospitals to distribute money, provisions, and clothing. She and
her sister Maggie spent many hours knitting, both for the soldiers
and for members of the Davis and Howell families.[43]

At the Confederate White House, Christmas of 1862 and the
New Year that followed were not as festive as usual because the

President was absent on a long morale-boosting trip to Tennessee and Mississippi. Varina must have been pleased by a letter of December 15 from Chattanooga, which closed with the affectionate lines: "Kiss my dear children for their loving Father. . . . None can equal their charms, nor can any compare with my own long worshipped Winnie—

> She is na my ain Lassie
> Though fair the lassie be
> For well ken I my ain lassie
> By the kind love in her eye*

. . . . Ever affectionately, your Husband."[44]

It was not often that Davis broke into poetry, even when addressing his beloved wife.

January and February of 1863 were months of exceptional social activity for the Davises. This was due in large part to the fact that the Chesnuts had as their house guests during this period the beautiful Preston sisters from South Carolina, Mary and Sally ("Buck"), and they became the centers of much entertaining. President Davis gave a breakfast for Mrs. Chesnut and her guests, and Mrs. Davis was hostess at a musical matinee. Afterward, Mrs. Chesnut was queried so closely by acquaintances as to what she and other guests did at the White House functions that she blurted,

---

*The quotation is from a "Song" of the poet Robert Burns, a favorite of President Davis. The lines, as Burns wrote them, were:
> O this is no my ain lassie,
>   Fair tho' the lassie be;
> Weel ken I my ain lassie,
>   Kind love is in her e'e.

See James Kinsley, ed., *The Poems and Songs of Robert Burns* (Oxford, 1968), II, 799.

"We danced on the tight rope." This remark, when reported to Varina, brought from the First Lady the whispered admonition, "Have mercy, dear. Never say that again. They will believe you. You do not know this Richmond. They swallow scandal with such wide open mouths. And their easy credulity is such that next winter they will have the exact length of our petticoats and describe the kind of spangles we were sprinkled with."[45]

In mid-March 1863, Mrs. Davis was called to Montgomery by the fatal illness of her father. When she returned to Richmond after the funeral, she was confronted by a series of crises. First was a bread riot of April 2, during which several hundred citizens, mostly women and children, began a raid on bakeries, stores, and shops; the revolt was quelled by the President mounting a wagon and threatening to have the mob shot by his military escort. Shortly afterward, Davis was stricken with an attack of fever and bronchitis which incapacitated him for several weeks. Early in May the city was imperilled by Stoneman's raiders. During the emergency Varina asked Mrs. Chesnut to spend the night at the White House. The next morning Mary saw the President "still feeble and pale from his illness" ride off with aides as if in search of the Federals, but by that time the danger had passed.[46] Soon came the report of Lee's great victory at Chancellorsville and of the wounding of Stonewall Jackson. The following week Varina and the President went to the Governor's mansion to pay respects to the dead hero.

The double disaster of Gettysburg and Vicksburg enhanced the gloom that hung over Richmond after Jackson's death. The loss of Vicksburg, which was especially galling to Davis, caused a rekindling of antagonism between the President and General Joe Johnston, each of whom blamed the other for the catastrophe. The wives did not enter openly into the controversy, but Lydia Johnston revealed the depth of her hatred when she wrote Charlotte Wigfall on August 2: "I feel now nothing can ever make me forgive either of them [the Davises]. When I looked at my dear old husband's gray head & careworn face & felt how many of those tokens of trouble that man and woman have planted there, I could almost have asked God to punish them. . . . It is not this war that has broken up my home & almost my heart, but the vengeance of one wicked man.''[47]

In the fall of 1863 Varina was deprived of the companionship of her husband while he made a month's trip through the South to restore harmony among quarreling leaders, strengthen defenses, and bolster morale. During the separation Varina experienced a lapse of spirit, but she was brighter by the time Davis returned home, if not before. On November 30 Mary Chesnut noted in her diary: "I gave a party. . . . Mrs. Davis [was] very witty.''[48] The President spent a quiet Christmas with his family. On New Year's Day 1864, he and Varina gave what the Richmond *Whig* described as "the annual reception of the public." From noon until 3:00 P.M. host and hostess greeted scores of "Ladies and gentlemen, officers and civilians." According to the *Whig* reporter, "the reception was conducted in the approved Republican style, and passed off in a manner satisfactory to all.''[49]

The success of the New Year's affair, and the Davises' desire to improve public relations encouraged them to initiate a series of weekly receptions. But these were soon discontinued, probably because of the danger incurred by admitting throngs of strangers to the Davis residence. Someone tried to burn the White House during the reception of January 19. The fire may have been started by Henry, the Davis butler, who the next day ran off to the Yankees. The President now seemed to be having difficulty keeping Negro help. Previously, a White House coachman and barber had absconded and soon Betsy, Varina's mulatto maid, was to disappear, lured away apparently by Federal gold.

Discontinuance of White House functions did not interfere with the gay social season enjoyed by residents of Richmond in the early months of 1864. The major events of the season, both attended by the Davises, were a benefit charade (in which eight-year-old Maggie Davis had a part) given at the home of Senator and Mrs. Thomas J. Semmes in January, and an amateur presentation in February of Sheridan's play "The Rivals" at the home of Colonel and Mrs. Joseph Ives. On these and other occasions the Davises mingled pleasantly with an assortment of the Confederacy's military, political, and social leaders, including General Hood and the Prestons. Mary Chesnut, Varina Davis, and others lent their aid to Hood in his unlucky courtship of Sally Preston. He had better luck in his efforts to ingratiate himself with the President, from whom he received promotion first to lieutenant general and later to full general. Varina may not have shared her husband's high appraisal of Hood. On December 14, 1863, Mrs. Chesnut wrote that "Mrs. Davis . . . rates Fitzhugh Lee far above Hood." Later entries in the Chesnut diary indicate that Varina thought Hood overzealous in his wooing of Sally Preston.[50]

As the season for renewal of active military operations approached, Davis suffered increasingly from insomnia and loss of appetite. To beguile him into eating, Varina renewed her practice of taking a warm snack to his office. On April 30, just as she uncovered the food basket, a servant dashed into the Executive Office with the news that five-year-old Joe Davis had fallen from the White House balcony to a brick pavement some thirty feet below. The frightened parents rushed home to find their beloved child dying. An officer who reached the scene before the arrival of the Davises reported: "We at once ran in and found the little fellow . . . in the arms of a Negro man, insensible and almost dead . . . Mr. and Mrs. Davis came in while we held the little fellow, rubbing him. She relieved herself in a flood of tears, and wild lamentations, he knelt by his side and clasped the dying boy's hands in his own thin, attenuated fingers. As he then held his hands and watched the boy die such a look of petrified . . . anguish I never saw."[51]

The child apparently had slipped away from his nurse and lost his footing while climbing over a bannister. In her memoir Varina recalled: "This child was Mr. Davis's hope and greatest joy in life.

At intervals, he ejaculated, 'Not mine, oh, Lord, but thine'. A courier came with a dispatch. He took it, held it open for some moments and looked at me fixedly, saying, 'Did you tell me what was in it?' I saw his mind was momentarily paralyzed by the blow, but at last he tried to write an answer and then called out in a heart-broken tone, 'I must have this day with my little child.' Somebody took the dispatch to General Cooper and left us alone with our dead.'' This was the child who, one night not long before the fatal fall, had pushed his way through a crowd of visitors and insisted upon saying his evening prayer at the President's knee.[52]

On June 27, 1864, less than two months after Joe's death, Varina gave birth to her sixth and last child, a girl. She was named Varina Anne, but during her infancy her parents called her "Piecake." Later, she was generally known as "Winnie." "Piecake's" winsome ways did much to ease the pain of losing Joe and to make more tolerable the criticism heaped upon the President by a war-weary people engulfed in a tide of deprivation and death and confronted by a future that seemed almost devoid of hope. Varina felt the pinch of scarcity to a degree that caused her to sell her carriage horses. Anonymous friends bought the animals and sent them back to her, but she still had difficulty providing feed for them.

The President in September, after the fall of Atlanta, left the capital for another trip through the South to combat the mounting wave of defeatism. Mrs. Chesnut entertained him in Columbia, South Carolina, and early in October Varina wrote a letter of appreciation to her in which she stated: ''It did his heart good to see your reserved General and you once more. . . . We are in a sad and anxious state here now. The dead come in, the living do not go out so fast. However, we hope all things and trust in God. . . . Strictly between us, things look very anxious here. . . . I am so constantly depressed that I dread writing, for penned lines betray our feelings despite every care.'' Varina lightened the gloom of these comments by remarking: ''And now, dear friend, I must brag a little about my baby. She is so soft, so good, and so very lady-like, and knows me very well. She is white as a lily, and has such exquisite hands and feet, and such bright blue eyes."[53]

Later that fall Varina wrote Mrs. Chesnut: "I am so tired [of] hoping, fearing and being disappointed that I have made up my mind not to be disconsolate even though thieves break through and steal. . . . The temper of Congress is less vicious, but more concerted in its hostile action. . . . People do not snub me any longer, for it was only while the lion was dying that he was kicked; dead, he was beneath contempt. Not to say I am worthy to be called a lion, nor are the people here asses. Scandal is rife here."*[54]

Sherman's capture of Savannah, Hood's disastrous defeat in Tennessee, and a general worsening of conditions throughout the South made Christmas of 1864 a gloomy time for the people of the Confederacy. The Davises, like most parents in the beleaguered South, put up as good a front as possible for their children and with reasonably good results. Children's stockings were stuffed with molasses candy, ginger snaps, and homemade toys such as spinning tops fashioned from large buttons and kitchen matches, balls "of worsted rags wound hard and covered with old gloves," and paper dolls. After distribution of the gifts on Christmas morning, the family walked to St. Paul's Church for holiday worship and then came home to a meal featuring delicacies that only the most privileged Confederates could afford. These included turkey, roast beef, mince pie, plum pudding, and "a spun sugar hen, life-size on a nest full of blanc mange eggs."[55]

Varina began the New Year by attending church with her husband. Both needed spiritual solace. As the Confederacy's fortune declined, they were subjected to vehement denunciations in the press and among the people. On January 17, 1865, Mrs. H. L. Clay, wife of an officer stationed in Richmond, wrote her sisters:

*Both of the letters to Mrs. Chesnut quoted here are from the manuscript Chesnut diary.

"Everybody is down upon Mr. Davis. You never read in all your life such articles as comes out in the Examiner. He looks badly —old, grey & wrinkled. . . . I am truly sor[r]y for him. The Madam told Mr. C. that she had 'a great deal rather *die* than live,' &c, &c. But she is enormously fat, & very cross, & ill-tempered."[56] Varina was said to have been greatly offended when Congress, late in January 1865, passed a law which required the President to appoint a general-in-chief to command all the military forces. Senator Louis T. Wigfall wrote Joseph E. Johnston, "Mrs. Jeff is open in her denunciations."[57] Edward Pollard, in his biography of the Confederate President, states that when in February Senator Gustavus Henry of Tennessee made a social call at the White House, Mrs. Davis angrily accused him of turning against her husband in supporting the legislation that resulted in Lee's elevation to highest command. When Henry replied that Congress had only acted in accordance with the will of the people, Varina warmly retorted: "I think I am the person to advise Mr. Davis; and if I were he, I would die or be hung before I would submit to the humiliation that Congress intended him."[58] Pollard's anti-Davis bias may have caused him to distort the account of Varina's behavior, but she could be very caustic when greatly upset, as she obviously was on this occasion.

After Congress adjourned on March 18, most of the members hastened home to look after their families. Amidst the gloom that pervaded the capital and the South, the Davises maintained an appearance of confidence and calm. Varina, more realistic than her husband, prepared for the inevitable by selling clothing, silver, china, and other possessions, and making arrangements to convert into gold the Confederate dollars realized from the sales. About a week before the fall of Richmond, the President told his wife that she and the children must head southward for safety. She made a strong protest, but to no avail. As Varina recalled events twenty-five years later: "He said for the future his headquarters must be in the field and that our presence would only embarrass and grieve

instead of comforting him. . . . He was very much affected and said
'If I live you can come to me when the struggle is ended, but I do
not expect to survive the destruction of constitutional liberty'."
The President gave his wife a small pistol and showed her how to
use it.[59]

On a night near the end of March, Varina with her four children
and her sister Maggie boarded a train and began a long trip that was
to take them by various modes of transportation through North and
South Carolina into Georgia. Davis fled the capital on April 2.
Anxious and affectionate messages passed between husband and
wife during the next month, but they were not reunited until a few
days before their capture at Irwinsville, Georgia, on May 10.

May 10, 1865, marks the end of Varina's incumbency as First
Lady of the Confederacy. An objective appraisal of her performance in that role is difficult. She kept no diary, and only a few of
the letters that she wrote during the war have been preserved. The
two-volume memoir that she completed in 1890 is concerned
mainly with her husband and consists in large part of long quotations from his publication, *The Rise and Fall of the Confederate
Government*. The comments that she makes about herself in the
memoir are revealing, but in using them allowance has to be made
for bias and the failure of memory. What her Confederate contem-
poraries wrote about her also tends to be distorted, for she aroused
extreme reactions—either strong admiration or intense antipathy.
But a careful weighing of available evidence indicates that she
measured up well as the Confederacy's First Lady. The first of her
strong attributes was that she was well-informed. Judge Winchester and Madame Grelaud gave her a good foundation in fundamen-
tals, which she built on by reading and by soaking up information
from sophisticated associates, such as Mary Chesnut, the John S.
Preston family (who had lived abroad for four years preceding the
war), John C. Breckinridge, Judah P. Benjamin, Burton Harrison,
and Jefferson Davis.

A second asset was her sociability. She liked people, especially

**Varina Howell at 18,
about the time she married Jefferson Davis**

Varina and Jefferson Davis as bride and groom in 1845

Courtesy of Mrs. John W. Stewart

Varina Howell Davis as First Lady of the Confederacy

Courtesy of Museum of the Confederacy, Richmond, Virginia.

Winnie Davis, youngest child of President and Mrs. Jefferson Davis. Born in Confederate White House, Richmond, Virginia, June 27, 1864, and known as "The Daughter of the Confederacy."

Children of Jefferson and Varina Davis as exiles. Photo taken by William Notman, in Toronto, Canada, in 1866 or 1867. Children, left to right, and dates of their birth: Jefferson, Jr., 1857; Maggie, 1855; Winnie, 1864; William Howell, 1861.

Courtesy of Museum of the Confederacy, Richmond, Virginia

Jefferson Davis and his wife Varina.
Photo taken about 1868.

Courtesy of Museum of the Confederacy, Richmond,
Virginia

intelligent people, and she was able to hold her own in conversation with the leading lights of the Confederacy. She had a special liking for young folk, probably because of her own youth—she was only thirty-five when the war began. In addition, she had a natural vibrancy of spirit that made her feel at home with Maggie Howell, Constance Cary, Johnny Chesnut, Burton Harrison, and other persons in their late teens or early twenties.

Still another quality that won the admiration of most of her friends was her charm. Her good looks, her easy manner, and her warm smile gave her an appeal exceeding that of most of her associates. All of these attributes, combined with her good taste, her ready wit, and her consummate poise, enabled her to preside graciously and effectively over social functions large and small, formal or informal. An English correspondent who attended a White House levee early in 1864 paid Varina this compliment: "That lady is by no means an ordinary woman. Her style is very much that of the period of George the Third. . . . She is a stately woman, with a brunette complexion and eyes full of brilliance, tenderness and intelligence. Her manners are very agreeable but touched with a repose that even though carried to almost sadness savors very much of the grand."[60]

One of her shortcomings was hypersensitiveness, especially in matters concerning her husband. She found it difficult to tolerate any criticism of him or to feel or act kindly toward the person making the criticism. Another fault was an explosive temper, which she usually held under control. A glimpse of what it was like when it got out of hand was given by William W. Blackford's description of an incident he observed in 1861: "Walking along the streets one day I happened to be behind a lady as she reached a cross street. A negro boy coming along the cross street mounted on a beautiful blooded horse which he was, after the manner of his kind when unobserved, fretting and jerking to make him prance. The lady burst out into a fury of invective, the like of which I never before heard from a lady's lips, and made the groom dismount and lead the horse away. It was Mrs. Jeff Davis, and the groom and the horse belonged to the President's stables.''[61] Another instance of Varina's ill temper was cited by Mrs. Chesnut in the original, unpublished version of her diary, in an entry for July 23, 1861: "Met Trescott [William H. Trescot, assistant secretary of state, 1860]. Went with him to Mrs. Davis' room. She treated him to a quantity of indecent abuse & when we left the room he said she was the vulgarest woman he ever knew.''

Mrs. Davis was not always as tactful as she should have been, especially when dealing with what she and Mrs. Chesnut regarded as Richmond's "solemn, ponderous society.'' At a dinner party the wife of a general dolefully told how the drawers intended for one of her husband's regiments had been ruined by the volunteer seamstresses who used the pattern for the right leg only when cutting the cloth. While all the other ladies expressed horror at so costly a blunder, Varina, struck by the humor of the incident, let out a guffaw that shocked and offended her associates. There were other times when the volatile Varina reacted with hearty laughs to situations which serious-minded companions thought to be devoid of humor. She was a straight-forward, candid person and flattery seemed alien to her nature. Her humor sometimes had a cutting edge and her forthrightness occasionally was carried to extremes. T. C. DeLeon, a perceptive journalist who knew and liked her, wrote long after the war: "Varina Howell Davis preferred the straight road to the tortuous bypath. She was naturally a frank though not a blunt woman, and her bent was to kindliness and charity. Sharp tongue she had, when set that way and the need came to use it; and her wide knowledge of people and things sometimes made that use dangerous to offenders.''[62]

Appraisal of Varina's role as First Lady of the Confederacy would be incomplete without considering the nature and extent of her influence on the President. Edward Pollard, harsh critic of the President during and after the war, stated in his biography of Davis: "This man who could set his face as flint against the counsels of the intelligent was as wax in the hands of his wife.''[63] DeLeon, on the other hand, labeled as ''silly tales'' the reports of Varina ''sowing dissension in the cabinet and being behind the too frequent changes in the heads of the government.''[64] Both of these comments doubtless have some validity. Varina was thoroughly devoted to her husband and deeply interested in all of his activities. She tried to maintain an atmosphere at home that would be most conducive to his health and happiness. She avoided extravagances in dress and in running the household. She did what she could to overcome his aversion to social activities, but she did not press unduly for the continuance of public receptions when he insisted that these interfered with his work or were injurious to his health. She sought to compensate for dearth of large-scale entertaining by arranging small and informal get-togethers with their most pleasant associates.

One of the most frequent visitors at the White House was Judah P. Benjamin, the man above all others on whom the President leaned for advice and assistance. Varina developed a warm friendship with Benjamin early in the war, and it seems reasonable to conclude that her esteem of this cabinet member stemmed from the great trust reposed in him by the President. In 1898 Varina told the British journalist Francis Lawley that Benjamin sometimes explained state papers to her and that ''He never put on a manner of reserve towards me. . . . Of what he knew I must be cognizant, he spoke freely when alone with me.''[65] This statement shows that Varina had a good opportunity for voicing her opinions on affairs of state; to what extent she made use of it can only be surmised.

It is clear that Varina had firm opinions about political affairs and a willingness to pass them on to men of influence. In a letter in the spring of 1865 to General John S. Preston, head of the Bureau of Conscription, she wrote:

You know I am a revolutionary, therefore, will excuse the expression of a habitude of free thought to me so dear and intimate. Our Constitution is framed for peace and nothing but a pure intelligence could be governed by it in times when the selfishness of man is so severely tested. . . . A strict construction of our Constitution is incompatible with the successful prosecution of a war. . . . I am disheartened with popular sovereignty, still more with state sovereignty. . . . However, if we have erred in Judgement we had a right to indulge our own theories of government and I do not regret the separation.[66]

A most revealing commentary on Varina's attempts to influence her husband is her statement to him in a letter of April 7, 1865, when he was trying to get to the Trans-Mississippi Department for continuation of the war: "Though I know you do not like my interference let me entreat you not to send B[raxton] B[ragg] to command there. I am satisfied that the country will be ruined by its intestine feuds if you do. . . . If I am intrusive forgive me for the sake of the love which impels me but pray long and fervently before you decide to do it."[67] This statement proves conclusively that Varina had previously offered advice to the President concerning matters of public policy and that he had manifested his disapproval—but not in such a manner as to preclude her making one last effort to influence him in a major appointment.

In view of what is known of the personalities and prior relationships of the President and Varina, it is impossible to accept Pollard's view that Davis "was as wax in the hands of his wife." He was too strong-willed, too smart, and too opinionated to be dominated by anyone. Varina, however, shared too many of these same qualities to permit her to be content with a purely passive role. She was completely willing to devote major emphasis to domestic duties. But it is reasonable to assume that views on public men and policy expressed to Mrs. Chesnut and other friends were shared with the man whose children she bore, whose speeches she copied, and whose respect and affection she commanded. With her intelligence and charm, she probably influenced him far more than he realized. But she had profound respect for him, and she was happy to recognize him as head of house and chief of state.

The future looked very dark for Varina and her husband on May 10, 1865, as their Federal captors escorted them from Irwinsville toward Macon. Just before Davis was apprehended by the Northern cavalrymen, he had picked up his wife's rain cape in the semi-darkness, thinking it was his own, and when he could not find his hat, Varina had thrown her shawl over his head to protect him from the rain. His attirement in his wife's cape and shawl when the Federals seized him gave rise to the report that he had disguised himself as a woman in an effort to elude his pursuers. Northern papers ridiculed him by picturing him wearing hoop skirt and petticoat. This widely circulated canard was humiliating to the prisoners. En route to Macon Davis learned that he had been charged with complicity in the assassination of Lincoln and that President Andrew Johnson had offered $100,000 for his capture. At Macon the Davises, along with Clement and Virginia Clay, were placed in the custody of General James H. Wilson, who sent them by train to Augusta. There they were joined by another group of prisoners, which included Vice-President Alexander Stephens. The party proceeded by way of Savannah to Port Royal. There they boarded the ocean steamer, the *William P. Clyde*, which took them to Fort Monroe where Davis and Clay were imprisoned. Varina begged to accompany her husband when he was removed from the *Clyde*, but to no avail. "We parted in silence," she wrote in her memoir. "As the tug bore him away from the ship, he stood with bared head . . . and as we looked, as we thought our last [time] upon his stately form and knightly bearing, he seemed a man of another and higher race."[68]

Varina with her four children and Maggie Howell returned to Savannah on the *Clyde*. There she read in a newspaper that General Nelson A. Miles, the commandant at Fort Monroe, had put her husband in shackles, and this almost drove her insane. Later she learned that the chains had been removed but that he was still kept in close confinement in a damp cell with a light constantly shining in his eye. She was in agony for fear that he would be blinded by the glare and killed or driven mad by confinement. She began a letter-writing campaign on his behalf to Francis P. Blair, Montgomery Meigs, Horace Greeley, Andrew Johnson, and many others. Johnson, who had never forgotten what he considered an insult from Davis when the two were in Congress in 1846,* did not reply. But Blair responded sympathetically and Greeley got a distinguished lawyer, George Shea, to assist another prominent New York attorney, Charles O'Conor, who in May 1865 volunteered to act as counsel for Davis.

For two months Varina remained virtually a prisoner in a Savannah hotel; later, in July 1865, she was allowed to move to Mill View, the plantation of a friend, George Schley, near Augusta, where she stayed until December. In the meantime she sent her mother and the three older children, ten-year-old Margaret, eight-year-old Jefferson, and three-year-old Billy to Montreal, Canada, where Margaret and Jeff were enrolled in Catholic boarding schools.

At Mill View Varina lived rent-free in a guest house, with her baby and an amiable Irish nurse, Mary Ahern, who was to care for little Winnie for more than ten years. Varina was reasonably comfortable at the Schleys, but she suffered acutely from loneliness, anxiety, and depression. Early in September she received a letter from her husband, the first that he had been allowed to write. Henceforth, correspondence with him was her greatest comfort. The letters evidence a deepening affection between Varina and her husband during their separation; they also indicate that Davis was stronger in adversity than was Varina. A principal reason seems to have been his greater reliance on Divine Providence. Varina was

---

*In a debate Davis spoke disparagingly of tailors, a group with which Johnson was identified as a young man.

deeply religious, but she found it impossible to love her enemies, especially those who were unkind to her husband, or to accept with a resignation comparable to his the changed circumstances that came with Confederate defeat. Her spirit sank almost to the breaking point in the fall and winter of 1865-1866. On November 13 she wrote: "The dreary, dreary days and weeks and months—I grow hard & sullen with sorrow. . . . If we are not to be reunited, may God take me to himself." On January 22, 1866, she poured out her affection and sorrow in a letter closing with the words: "If I have ever offended you, and I have been often willful and irritable, oh forgive your poor old wife for her great love's sake. . . . A lingering, longing, loving farewell to you, my precious good Husband."[69]

Things took a turn for the better in February when Varina received permission to leave Georgia. With Burton Harrison as escort and with free passes from the railroads, she, Winnie, and Mary Ahern headed for Canada by way of Louisiana and Mississippi. At stopovers along the way she was flooded with manifestations of kindness and solicitude for herself and her husband. From New Orleans, where she spent fifteen days and bought some new clothes, she wrote Jefferson that she was "overwhelmed by the love which everything of your name attracts." At Vicksburg she stopped to see her brother-in-law Joe, now staying at a boarding house and so hard-pressed for funds that Varina gave him $400. From Vicksburg she proceeded to New York for conferences with her husband's attorneys and then she went on to Montreal. From there on April 14, she sent a detailed report to her husband. Her mother was sick with bronchitis but the Davis children were hale and hearty: "Beautiful Billy," she added, was "fat as a little possum and so sweet and loving to his Mudder . . . our little Maggie fat but not rosy. . . ." Jeffy D. . . . "very healthy and much grown . . . fought a boy of sixteen for pretending to believe that you were in petticoats at your capture. . . . I told him your last message, and he seated himself in a chair, covered his face and

sobbed out, 'the dear dear fellow, will I ever see him again'. . . .
He has a number of English expressions.''[70]

Two weeks after Varina arrived in Montreal she heard a rumor
that Davis was dying. She immediately telegraphed President
Johnson: "Is it possible that you will keep me from my dying
husband? Can I come to see him?"[71] The request was granted and
on May 3 she arrived at Fort Monroe with Winnie. The reunion
was a happy one, though Varina was greatly troubled by her
husband's "shrunken form and glassy eyes," his vermin-infested
bed, his unappetizing food, the petty tyranny of the commandant,
General Nelson Miles, and the annoyance of the sentries' constant
tread. With the help of the prison surgeon, Dr. George Cooper,
Varina sent out reports indicating that Davis's poor treatment in
the prison was endangering his sanity and his life. These reports
inspired sympathetic editorials in Northern newspapers. Varina
also wrote President Johnson on her husband's behalf. Late in May
she went to Washington to see the President. Johnson received her
politely, but told her that the time was not ripe for freeing Davis,
and that his hands were tied by Radical opposition in Congress. He
suggested that the best course to follow was for Davis to write him
a letter asking for pardon. Varina told him that this her husband
would not do because it would amount to a confession of guilt.[72]

Meanwhile, Federal authorities, having concluded that they had
no grounds for charging Davis with complicity in Lincoln's assassination, had him indicted for treason in the United States Circuit
Court at Richmond. Davis's lawyers were hopeful that he would
be brought to trial in Richmond in June and exonerated, but the
district attorney ruled that the circuit court lacked jurisdiction.

Largely as a result of Varina's visit to Washington, Davis's
situation at Fort Monroe was greatly improved. He was allowed to
receive letters from friends, to walk about the fort, and to receive
more palatable food. In September 1866 Davis was permitted to
share a four-room apartment at the fort with his wife, his baby,
Mary Ahern, and two Negro servants. Life was further brightened

for the Davises by the visits of many old friends including former President Pierce. The greatest disappointment of that fall was a further postponement of Davis's trial until the following spring. In November Varina went to Canada to visit the Davis children and the Howells. Davis vetoed her proposal to bring the younger children to Fort Monroe on the ground that he did not want them to see him as a prisoner. But when she returned for Christmas she brought along their oldest daughter, Margaret Howell.

In March 1867 Varina went to Baltimore to renew efforts for Davis's release. She succeeded in persuading John W. Garrett, president of the Baltimore and Ohio Railroad, to see his good friend, Secretary of War Stanton, and plead for her husband's parole. This action brought quick and favorable results. On May 11, 1867, Davis was taken from Fort Monroe to Richmond, where two days later he was released on $100,000 bail bond signed by Horace Greeley, Gerrett Smith, and other leading Republicans. Davis remained subject to call for trial, but the call never came. He became a free man under President Johnson's general amnesty proclamation of December 25, 1868.

Davis's release from prison was the beginning of a new and different life for him and his family. It was a life marked by hopes and disappointments, by joys and sorrows, and by long separations and happy reunions. Shortage of money was a chronic problem. This posed a special difficulty for Varina, who was exceedingly ambitious for her children, especially for their education. Proper education, she felt, required travel and study in Europe.

Varina's first task was to get her family back together and help her husband recover his health. To this end she took him to Canada, where after a joyful reunion with his children and renewal of acquaintance with Confederate leaders, part of the family settled down in a hotel at Lennoxville, about 100 miles east of Montreal, and the older children enrolled in nearby schools. Varina tried to get her husband started on writing a history of the Confederacy, but he demurred on the ground that he could not "speak of my dead so soon." In the winter of 1867-1868, the Davises left their children with relatives and servants for a long trip to Cuba, New Orleans, Mississippi, and Virginia. Varina had hoped that return to the happier scenes of earlier years would revive her husband's drooping spirits, but the desolation and misery that he saw throughout the South had an opposite effect.[73]

Back in Canada, Varina, on July 6, 1868, wrote Howell Cobb: "Mr. Davis's health has not improved, he looks wretchedly and I think much of his indisposition is induced by his despair of getting some employment which will enable him to educate our children."[74] At her strong insistence Davis shortly afterward sailed with his family for Liverpool, where he hoped to establish a profitable connection as a cotton broker. The position failed to materialize, but the Davises put their sons in school near Liverpool and sent Maggie to a Catholic institution in Paris. Living mostly in London, Jefferson and Varina spent a year and a half in Europe. They made an extended trip to Paris and Davis on his own visited Switzerland, Scotland, and Wales. They were entertained often and sumptuously by European aristocrats who had been friendly to the Confederacy, and by Southern expatriates, including Judah P. Benjamin, John Slidell, and Dudley Mann. Davis's health improved during the European sojourn. Neither he nor Varina however, was willing to make a career of being entertained, and both were greatly concerned about financial security and the education of their children. Motherly instinct and her husband's absences led Varina to assume major responsibility for the rearing of their offspring. She ruled with a strong hand, but with abiding affection and with good results. When circumstances impelled her in 1869 to employ a governess to help her with the care and education of Maggie and Winnie, she wrote her husband: "I hope that I have met your views in all that I have done. . . . You are most generally generous in your silence when you disapprove, if you do."[75] He approved. Varina taught the girls piano and helped instruct them in French.

In the fall of 1869, Davis returned home and settled in Memphis to become president of the Carolina Insurance Company at an annual salary of $12,000. With his blessing Varina and the children remained in Europe until the fall of 1870. In April 1870, Maggie Howell married Karl Stoess, an Alsatian widower twenty years her senior who was in business in Liverpool. Varina wrote Davis shortly before the wedding that her sister was motivated by flattered vanity and that the affair was about to drive Varina mad.[76]

Varina was not happy about the prospect of living in Memphis, but once she arrived there, she won many friends and made a reasonably attractive home of a rented house on Court Street. She went to Baltimore in May 1871 to spend the summer in a cooler climate and to be with her three eldest children who were now in school there. During her absence Davis was occupied with his insurance business and with straightening out difficulties connected with the will of his brother Joe, who had died in the fall of 1870.

In the fall of 1871, the two Davis boys entered public school in Memphis and at Christmas the whole family was home for the first time in several years. The next fall brought tragedy when the lovable ten-year-old Billy died of diphtheria. The following year tragedy struck again in the failure of the Carolina Insurance Company. These troubles bore heavily on Varina and her husband, but deepened them spiritually and strengthened their affection and interdependence. Davis's departure for England in early 1874, to recoup his health and seek employment, led to a correspondence which was filled with the tenderest expressions of deep and continuing devotion between husband and wife.

Six months abroad improved Davis's health, but brought no employment. In the autumn of 1875, Varina's brother "Jeffy D." Howell, whom she loved very dearly in spite of his writing letters beginning with the salutation "My darling old Fat Sis," was drowned in the Pacific when the passenger ship he commanded collided with another vessel. Varina bore her sorrow in silence, sustained only by a faith that sometimes faltered and the certain knowledge of her husband's love. Her life was brightened by the marriage on January 1, 1876, of her daughter Maggie to J. Addison Hayes, a young Memphis banker who measured up well to her high standards of character and conduct. The big church wedding was a severe strain on the Davis's depleted resources, but Varina carried it off in a manner that reflected great credit on her persistence and resourcefulness.

In May 1876 Varina sailed with Davis and thirteen-year-old Winnie to England and Germany. Davis made the trip as head of the American department of a recently launched trading venture known as the International Chamber of Commerce and Mississippi Valley Society. This company, working through American and European departments and utilizing ships built in England, hoped to develop a thriving trade between the old and new worlds. The idea seemed promising on paper, but investors were skeptical of its soundness. Within a few months it became apparent that this venture, like all other businesses with which Davis had been associated, would end in failure. The shock was more than Varina could endure. In July she became critically ill with heart trouble and other ailments. Davis left her bedside long enough to complete arrangements for enrolling Winnie in a girls' boarding school in Carlsruhe, Germany. In November 1876, after visiting Winnie's school, Davis left his convalescent wife with Maggie Stoess in Liverpool and sailed for America.

Back home Davis decided to do what Varina and others had long been urging him to do—begin the writing of a history of the Confederacy. While he was visiting the Mississippi Coast looking for a quiet place to work, Mrs. Sarah Dorsey, a rich and cultured widow living at Beauvoir near Biloxi, offered him the use of an attractive cottage on her premises, along with quarters for Robert Brown, his Negro aide, and her services as amanuensis. Davis gratefully accepted. Mrs. Dorsey also proposed to give him and Robert their meals, but on Davis's insistence she accepted fifty dollars a month for their board.

With the assistance of Major W. T. Walthall, who was especially helpful in assembling the necessary materials, Davis, early in 1877, settled down to work in his quiet, congenial surroundings. In March his son Jeff, then twenty years of age, a lovable youth but something of a ne'er-do-well, came to live with him. In the summer his daughter Maggie and her husband, grieving over the loss of their first baby, came for a vacation in another Beauvoir cottage.

Davis's principal worry was Varina, who was still in Europe, staying much of the time with her sister Margaret in Liverpool and keeping always in close touch with Winnie. She traveled some, but wrote her husband repeatedly that she did not feel well enough to undertake the long trip home. Although she expressed an earnest desire to regain enough strength to be useful, she revealed a lingering fear that she would never be healthy again.

Davis's reports of Mrs. Dorsey's kindnesses and helpfulness aroused Varina's jealousy and on September 9, 1877, she wrote:

> I am sorry not to have written to Mrs. Dorsey. . . . Nothing on earth would pain me like living in that kind of community in her house. . . . I am grateful for her kindness to you and my children, but do not desire to be under any more obligation to her. When people here ask me what part of your book she is writing, and such like things I feel aggravated nearly to death. Of course she must have given out the impression . . . [else] no one would have known she wrote at your dictation even, still less would it have come out in the newspapers. I have avoided mentioning her in my letters, for I felt too angry at the last squib in an illustrated paper to be reasonable.[77]

Soon after writing this letter, Varina found the strength to head home. But she went to Memphis instead of Beauvoir. Davis traveled to Memphis to see her in November, but he was unable to persuade her to return with him to the Mississippi Coast, a place where she had spent happy summers in the 1850s. While she tarried in Memphis she made helpful suggestions concerning his history. Uppermost in her mind, however, was Mrs. Dorsey. In April 1878 she wrote: "Do not, please do not let Mrs. Dorsey come to see me. I cannot see her and do not desire ever to do so again, beside[s] I do not wish to be uncivil & embarrass you and would certainly be so against my will. Let us agree to disagree about her and I will bear my separation from you as I have the last six months."[78] Interestingly, Varina made no mention of how her husband might bear separation from her.

Davis dealt patiently with his high-strung wife and kept gently reminding her of his need of her companionship and help. She finally joined him at Beauvoir in the summer of 1878 and remained with him there most of the time until his death. Her situation was eased considerably when Mrs. Dorsey died of cancer in 1879. Beauvoir was bequeathed to Davis, but he insisted on paying the estate the full purchase price of $5,500 to which he had committed himself before Mrs. Dorsey's death.

In the meantime the Davises had experienced another great personal calamity in the loss of their fourth, and last, son. Jefferson, Jr., died in Memphis of yellow fever on October 16, 1878. This tragedy prostrated Varina with "brain fever," leaving her critically ill for more than two weeks. Both she and her husband found respite from their grief by concentrating on his history of the Confederacy. Varina not only served as amanuensis, but also drew on her prodigious memory to provide many details and gave valuable suggestions for the assessment of people and events. The work, completed in the spring of 1881, was published the following June in two volumes under the title *The Rise and Fall of the*

Confederate Government. Varina's reaction to finishing the history, as given in a note to Winnie, was: "Well, dear love, the book is done & coming out—'whoop la'."

The Davises celebrated completion of the history with a trip to Europe. When they reached Paris in September, Winnie, who had completed five years of schooling at Carlsruhe, was there to meet them. After two months in France, devoted largely to visiting, shopping, and relaxing, all three Davises in November returned to America. Winnie's presence at Beauvoir brought much pleasure to her parents. At sixteen she was an intelligent, attractive, girl, possessing a personality that endeared her to all who knew her. She and her father were especially companionable, and to her Varina entrusted some of the reading and writing that she had previously done for him, while Varina devoted more time to gardening and to entertaining the many guests who called at Beauvoir. Since she never learned to love Beauvoir, she was happy occasionally to leave Jefferson with Winnie while she visited Memphis and New Orleans.

In October 1882, her brother Becket, who had served creditably as a Confederate naval officer on the *Alabama*, but who failed in all his postwar activities, died at forty-two while acting as overseer at Brierfield. Two years later her last surviving brother, William F. Howell, died in San Francisco; his life as a civilian had also been a succession of failures.

In 1885 Varina stayed at Beauvoir with her daughter Maggie and her three grandchildren, while Winnie accompanied Jefferson on a triumphal speaking trip to Alabama and Georgia. At Atlanta General John B. Gordon brought hundreds of old soldiers to their feet screaming the Rebel yell when he introduced Winnie as the "Daughter of the Confederacy." The next year Varina, Maggie, and Winnie all went with Davis to the grand reunion of Confederate veterans at Macon, Georgia. The trip, made in a special railway coach, was an exhausting experience, but Varina must have been thrilled by the tremendous ovations given to her husband and his family all along the way.

Mary Chesnut's death in 1886 brought from Varina the comment: "My old friends are dropping off very fast, and infirmities are accumulating upon me . . . but I most certainly do not want to die, and would see the world if I could but only in an impersonal way."[79]

She was able to see some of the world vicariously through Winnie who made several trips to Richmond, New York, and other Eastern cities in the late 1880s. At Syracuse in 1887 Winnie met Alfred Wilkinson, Jr., a twenty-eight-year-old lawyer of good family and exceptional attractiveness. It was a case of love at first sight. Winnie, fearful of her parents' reaction to her romance with a Yankee whose grandfather had been a prominent abolitionist, did not tell them of it until Wilkinson came to Beauvoir in September 1888 to ask for her hand. At first Jefferson refused, but as Wilkinson stayed on as a guest, Davis learned to like him and to appreciate the genuineness of Winnie's affection for him. After Wilkinson's return to New York, Davis reluctantly assented to the betrothal and Winnie proudly announced it to a few close friends. Varina, who was even more strongly opposed to the match than her husband, made some inquiries about Wilkinson's financial status which convinced her that he was not as well off as he claimed. When the report leaked out that the "Daughter of the Confederacy" was engaged to a Northerner, angry letters came to Beauvoir. This vehement protest and Winnie's realization that her insistence on marrying Wilkinson was causing pain to her parents upset the sensitive young woman and caused a serious decline in her health. In the fall of 1889 she sailed for Europe to think over her situation and try to regain wholeness of body and mind.

After Winnie's departure, her father, then eighty-one, left Beauvoir to visit Brierfield. En route to the plantation he caught a severe cold which developed into bronchitis. He became so ill after

reaching Brierfield that the overseer telegraphed Varina and put
the sick man on a boat bound for New Orleans. Varina, who had
started upriver, met and boarded the boat bearing her husband and
accompanied him to New Orleans. A doctor who met the steamer
at the dock stated that Davis was too sick to go to Beauvoir. He was
taken instead to the residence of a friend where a consulting
physician confirmed the diagnosis of acute bronchitis complicated
by malaria. He lingered for nearly three weeks while Varina kept
almost constant vigil by his bedside. He spoke often with her and
assured her that he had no fear of death. Early on the morning of
December 6 he sank quietly into final repose. Varina, overcome
with weariness and grief, gave way to profuse weeping until she
was relieved by a sedative. Telegrams were sent to Winnie in Paris
and to Maggie, who in 1885 had moved to Colorado Springs. That
night the body was borne to the New Orleans City Hall, where for
the next three days it lay in state while thousands of people came to
pay their last respects. On the afternoon of December 11, Varina
stood with her daughter Maggie, her nephew General Joe Davis,
and the venerable and ever faithful Negro aide, Robert Brown, in
front of a multitude of Confederate veterans and others while her
husband's remains were laid to rest in Metairie Cemetery.

Varina did not by nature brood over the loss of a loved one.
Experience had taught her that the best way to surmount sorrow
was to throw herself unreservedly into an absorbing activity. Such
an escape she now found in preparing a memoir of her husband.
While gathering material for this work she did what she could to
rescue Winnie from the depths of depression into which she had
fallen on hearing of her father's death. Varina soon decided to
swallow her pride and accept Fred Wilkinson as a son-in-law. At
her suggestion Wilkinson went to Europe to see Winnie.

During his travel abroad Wilkinson wrote Varina letters expressing uncertainty about Winnie's prospects for recovery and their
doubts as to the wisdom of marriage. Despite this unhappy situation Varina, after Wilkinson's return in April 1890, gave formal

notice of the engagement. During the months following, Varina and Wilkinson quarreled over her prying into his affairs; in September 1890, after Winnie's return home, Wilkinson made another trip to Beauvoir which resulted in an amicable but sad termination of the engagement.

While Winnie brooded over her shattered romance, Varina pushed relentlessly forward toward completion of her memoir. Her drive and persistence amazed and exhausted John Dimitry, a New Orleans friend, and James Redpath, a prominent journalist who had helped her husband with his *Short History of the Confederate States*, as they worked with her in the final revision. Late in 1890 she went to New York to read proof, leaving Winnie at Beauvoir. Her intense exertion caused a flareup of her heart trouble and sent Winnie to New York to serve as nurse. Soon both patient and nurse became so ill that Maggie came from Colorado to take care of them.

Rest, and the appearance in the spring of *Jefferson Davis, Ex-President of the Confederate States: A Memoir by His Wife*, restored Varina's vigor and quickened her interest in life. The two-volume work, totaling 1,638 pages, was poorly put together, excessively laudatory in its treatment of Davis, and overly critical of those who opposed him. But the work contained some important information not to be found elsewhere, and those portions treating of the author's own experiences and impressions, especially those written from memory, had a candor and vigor that made for good reading. While she obviously sought to present her husband in the most favorable light, she occasionally made a comment which had the opposite effect. An example is her representing Davis as saying repeatedly during the Gettysburg campaign: "If I could take one wing and Lee the other, I think we could between us wrest a victory from those people."[80] It is surprising that a person of Varina's exceptional intelligence did not perceive the presumption of one whose reputation as a combat commander rested on the successful leadership of one small regiment at Buena Vista, placing himself

on the same level with the man who had led an army of 60,000 to
brilliant victories at Second Manassas and Chancellorsville.

The memoir was too long, disjointed, and biased to be appealing
to a large reading audience, and the publisher's bankruptcy soon
after its appearance prevented adequate promotion. Royalties were
very small. Little if any income could be expected from Beauvoir,
which Winnie inherited, or from Brierfield, which was encum-
bered by debt. Maggie gave Varina and Winnie some financial
assistance, and gifts came occasionally from anonymous friends.
But mother and daughter, confined to Beauvoir, were hard up and
lonely. Winnie's selection as Queen of Comus at Mardi Gras in
1892 provided a welcome diversion. Varina yearned, both for her
own and for Winnie's sake, for an intellectually stimulating and
financially rewarding atmosphere. Winnie had shown promise as a
writer and Varina's memoir made her anxious to develop her own
literary leanings. The Joseph Pulitzers were old friends, eager to
assist the Davises in any way possible. These and other considera-
tions impelled Varina in 1892 to move to New York, where she
and Winnie settled down in an apartment at the Marlborough
Hotel. Soon they renewed acquaintance with the Burton Harrisons
and other former Confederates who had achieved success in
Gotham. At first some Southerners were critical of Jefferson
Davis's widow and the "Daughter of the Confederacy" casting
their lot with money-grubbing Yankees. But Varina paid little
attention to the carping and it eventually subsided. She was hurt
more by the ill-tempered remarks made by Mississippians when in
1893 she permitted her husband's remains to be removed to Richmond. She said little at the time, but she wrote a long and harsh
letter justifying her action and left instructions that it be published
after her death.[81]

In 1893 mother and daughter moved to less expensive quarters
in the Gerard Hotel, and for Varina's health and comfort they
began to spend summers at Narragansett Pier. In 1896 they both
attended the Confederate reunion at Richmond where they re-

ceived a tremendous ovation. Varina held a reception at the White House of the Confederacy, which that year was opened as a museum. For several years Varina had received a modest income from articles she contributed to the New York *Sunday World*, and Winnie realized small returns from reviews and from advances on her novels. Partly to obtain material for further writing but mainly to restore her failing health, Winnie spent the spring of 1898 abroad. She showed little improvement when she returned in May and she gradually wasted away from malnutrition and indigestion. On September 18, 1898 she died at the age of 33 of what her doctors called malarial gastritis.

Varina, strong of heart and accustomed to sorrow, accepted Winnie's passing with remarkable calm. She now focused her affections on Maggie and her grandchildren, two of whom came to New York to brighten the Christmas following Winnie's death.

As Varina grew older, her attitude softened toward some of her former foes. In 1893 she had a cordial meeting with Julia Dent Grant at West Point; in 1901 she wrote a favorable commentary on General Grant for the New York *Sunday World*. But her tolerance never grew to the point of permitting kindly feelings toward Yankee Generals Miles, Butler, and Sherman, or to Confederates Joe Johnston and Beauregard. After she sold Beauvoir for ten thousand dollars to the United Confederate Veterans in 1902 and a proposal was made to name rooms for various Southern generals, she emphatically stated that Joe Johnston and Beauregard should be excluded from those so honored.

She remained a staunch Confederate as long as she lived. In public meetings and in private correspondence, she was always ready to refute any aspersions cast upon those who had supported the Lost Cause. But she never permitted herself to become en-chained to the past. She was an avid reader of the newspapers and was consistently interested in current affairs. In view of her activist role with respect to things past and present, it seems strange that she opposed woman's suffrage ("A woman is no less a citizen because she has no vote, and can a good citizen have a higher duty than fitting a child to be the worthy head of a family?''), and was open in declaring her belief in the mental superiority of males.[82]

As the years passed, Varina grew heavier of body and spent more and more time in bed. But her mind remained alert and her talk never lost any of its pungency and sparkle. In both her conversation and her correspondence, she showed an amazing breadth of knowledge and a profound understanding of human nature. One of the highest tributes to her prowess as a conversationalist and her magnetism as a person was that paid by Professor John W. Burgess, who visited her often during their summers in Vermont: ''She charmed everybody in that old abolitionist state. . . . Most of the prominent men . . . paid her court and were all won by her courtesy, her kindness and her brilliant conversation.''[83] A similar accolade was accorded her by her grandson, whose name had been legally changed to Jefferson Hayes-Davis to carry on that of his mother's famous father and who often brought his Princeton friends to Varina's apartment for Sunday afternoon tea: ''They would rather spend their time with Mrs. Davis than go out in New York. Young and old were fascinated by her interesting, sprightly conversation.''[84]

In moving from the Gerard to the Majestic Hotel in October 1906, Varina caught a cold that developed into pneumonia. Two weeks later, on October 16, in the presence of Maggie, Maggie's family, and a few close friends, she repeated the scripture ''Oh Lord in thee have I trusted, let me not be confounded,'' and quietly breathed her last. The verse that she quoted was peculiarly appropriate. In her youth she had suffered from uncertainties and in maturity she made many mistakes and experienced numerous sorrows, disappointments, and frustrations. But she grew stronger with the passing of years, and her passion for orderliness combined with her imperious will to make her the dominant influence in the circles in which she moved. Neither in youth nor in later years was Varina confounded; even death did not end her influence for order.

Her military funeral in Richmond was governed in every detail by precise directions that she had given to Maggie earlier. Although she did not dictate her epitaph, she would have approved the words selected by her surviving daughter: ''Beloved and faithful wife of Jefferson Davis and devoted mother of his children.''[85]

4

Women of the Lost Cause

"Hurrah for the ladies! They are the soul of the war," wrote an Alabama soldier to a kinsman in 1863.[1] A similiar view was expressed by an Englishman who toured America in 1863, and who in a chapter on "Secesh Women" wrote: "I question whether either ancient or modern history can furnish an example of a conflict which was so much of a 'woman's war' as this. The bitterest, most vengeful of politicians in this ensanguined controversy are the ladies."[2] There can be no doubt of the correctness of these observations, for Southern women were among the most ardent advocates of secession. When hostilities erupted in the spring of 1861, mothers, wives, and sweethearts with few exceptions rallied to the support of the Southern cause. A Georgia mother wrote her son shortly after his enlistment: "I feel that you have gone forth in the name of the Lord. May He give strength to your arm [and] nerve to your heart to do your whole duty, and courage to fight the battle through. . . . Fain would I stand by your side and face the cannon ball, but this is denied me."[3]

Women put up a brave front when saying farewell to departing loved ones. An aristocratic lady of Fredericksburg wrote in her diary on June 3, 1861: "I saw some plain country people there telling their sons and husbands goodbye. I did not hear the first word of repining or grief, only encouragement to do their best and be of good service. One woman, after taking leave of her husband, said to two youths when telling them goodbye, 'Don't mind my tears, boys; they don't mean anything.' "[4]

When recruits proceeded to war zones by train, as most of them did, they were cheered at every hamlet and town by crowds of admiring women. And at stops along the way they were treated to food and drink by females of all ages. Private Robert Moore of the Seventeenth Mississippi Regiment wrote in his diary as he traveled toward Richmond in the summer of 1861:

> *June 12.* [At] Tuscumbia . . . saw a number of Ala. fairest daughters. They waved their hand flags & threw us flowers and fruit. . . . Arrived at Huntsville. . . . Had a splendid supper. . . . the ladies said hurrah for the Confederate Guards. . . . I will ever believe that their hearts are with Jeff Davis & the Southern Confederacy. . . . *June 15* . . . Left Knoxville at 6 o'clock A.M. . . . Passed through Greenville. . . . Jonesborough. . . . Union, at all of which places the ladies turned out & welcomed us. Received a boquet at Greenville with a note attached to it in which she requests me to write to her & says she would like to be a soldier's bride. . . . The ladies at Union had on aprons made like the flag of the Southern Confederacy. The boys were very much taken with them & begged for them. . . . *June 17.* . . . arrived at Lynchburg. . . . The citizens of the place gave us our breakfast & dinner but it was not very good.[5]

Lincoln's call for 75,000 troops on April 15, 1861, prompted an Alabama woman to go to the field where her two sons were laboring and to urge them to enlist for the duration of the conflict. Throughout the South young women showed their displeasure toward men who did not promptly volunteer for military service. Girls of Selma, Alabama, in response to an editor's suggestion, put on a "pout and sulk" campaign to stimulate volunteering. One of the town's belles announced that she would not keep company with a civilian. Another stated that she would become an old maid rather than marry a slacker. A third broke her engagement to a suitor who was slow to enlist and sent him a skirt and a petticoat with the message: "Wear these or volunteer."[6]

The patriotic fervor of some women soared to such heights that they sought to take up arms in their own defense. Mrs. Susan Lear of Virginia wrote Governor John Letcher in April 1861: "I for one feel able to protect a goodly number if I only had the means of defense. . . . Send me a *good* Musket, Rifle, or double barrel Shot Gun. I think I would prefer the latter as I am acquainted with its use. I believe, Sir, if a Regiment of Yankees were to come we [women] would drive them away or quell a servile insurrection."[7] A Georgia girl wrote in 1861 that she and her female friends had organized a unit for local defense. "The name of our company is the Bascom Home Guards," she stated; "we are all delighted with the idea of learning to shoot."[8]

In a few instances women disguised themselves as men and accompanied their husbands or sweethearts to camp. Usually their sex was soon detected and they were sent home. But at least two wives—Mrs. L. M. Blalock (who enlisted as Samuel Blalock) and Mrs. Amy Clarke—had considerable service with their spouses.[9] The Sandusky, Ohio, *Register* of December 12, 1864, reported: "One day last week one of the rebel officers . . . [imprisoned on] Johnson's Island gave birth to a 'bouncing boy.' This is the first instance of the father giving birth to a child, that we have heard of . . . it is [also] the first case of a woman in rebel service that we have heard of, though they are noted for goading their own men in[to] the army, and for using every artifice . . . to befog and befuddle some of our men."[10] Many women expressed annoyance at not being allowed to serve as soldiers. Sarah Morgan of Louisiana wrote in her diary the day the Yankees entered Baton Rouge: "O! if I was only a man! Then I could don the breeches and slay them with a will! If some few women were in the ranks, they could set the men an example they would not blush to follow."[11]

Feminine patriots assisted the South's armed forces in numerous ways. Many smuggled pistols, medicines, and other scarce items through the lines in their clothing or baggage. On August 29, 1861, Mary Chesnut noted in her diary: "All manner of things . . . come over the border under the huge hoop skirts now worn. . . . Not legs but arms are looked for under hoops."[12] Various Confederate generals benefited from information provided by women who served as spies. Laura Radcliffe and Antonia Ford were informers for both John Mosby and J. E. B. Stuart. Nancy Hart of West Virginia aided Stonewall Jackson in his Valley campaigns, and Rose Greenhow contributed to the Confederate victory at First Manassas by transmitting to Beauregard information obtained in Washington concerning McDowell's projected advance. Sixteen-year-old Emma Sansom of Alabama in 1864 helped General N. B. Forrest capture Colonel A. D. Streight by directing him to a ford across Black Creek after the Federals had burned the bridge which the Confederate leader had planned to use in his pursuit. The most famous of the girl spies was Belle Boyd of Martinsburg, West Virginia, who at great risk rode up and down the Shenandoah Valley gleaning information about Federal operations and passing it on to Ashby, Stuart, and Jackson.[13]

On the other hand, a few Southern women served as informers for the Union. Among them was the actress Pauline Cushman, a native of New Orleans, who in 1863 was arrested for espionage activities in Tennessee and was given a death sentence. She escaped and during the latter part of the war achieved considerable popularity on the Northern stage for her performances as a Yankee spy.[14]

Southern women also assisted the military effort by helping to care for sick and wounded soldiers. After great battles such as

Shiloh, Murfreesboro, Malvern Hill, Chickamauga, Chattanooga, and Spotsylvania, when casualties were crowded into railway stations, schools, hotels, and churches, women of nearby communities provided them with nourishment, blankets, bandages, and other necessities and did all they could to make them comfortable. In many instances ladies took wounded or sick soldiers into their homes and cared for them until they recovered, died, or were transferred to military hospitals. Women of Atlanta, Chattanooga, Macon, and many other cities established and administered wayside homes where ailing or needy soldiers could obtain food, shelter, and rest as they traveled through the South.

Relatively few women served as full-time nurses or administrators in Confederate hospitals, primarily because of the generally accepted view that such positions were the exclusive province of men. A few determined and resourceful women, breaking through the barrier of prejudice, made notable contributions to the care of sick and wounded soldiers. One of them was Ella King Newsom, a wealthy widow of Arkansas, who early in the war acquired training as a nurse in the Memphis City Hospital and who in December 1861 began to work among the wounded of General Albert Sidney Johnston's command at Bowling Green, Kentucky. She later served as superintendent of hospitals in Bowling Green, Nashville, Chattanooga, and Atlanta. She won wide acclaim both as nurse and as an administrator. The same may be said of Mrs. Arthur F. Hopkins, wife of the chief justice of Alabama who devoted her energies and fortune to the medical care of Alabama soldiers stationed in Virginia. She founded, funded, and administered several hospitals. She was twice wounded in the leg while working among the casualties at Seven Pines in 1862. The Alabama legislature gave her a vote of thanks and General Lee is said to have told her that she had done more for the South than all the women of her region.[15]

The only woman to hold a commission in the Confederate army was Sally L. Tompkins, who received a captaincy from President

Davis for her outstanding work in managing a Richmond hospital which she founded and which treated a total of 1,300 soldiers. Equally deserving of a commission was Phoebe Yates Pember, a cultured Jewish widow of Savannah, Georgia, who from December 1862 until the end of the war was chief matron of one of the five principal divisions of Richmond's Chimborazo Hospital, at that time the largest military hospital in the world. Nurses who got an especially high rating from Johnny Rebs were the Sisters of Charity, the Sisters of Mercy, and other groups of Catholic nuns who served in army hospitals throughout the Confederacy. They numbered less than two hundred, but their prior training as nurses, together with the dignity and devotion with which they performed their duties, enabled them to render a service that would have been a credit to a much larger group.[16]

Innumerable women aided the Confederate cause by making clothing for soldier relatives and friends. In the early months of the war a common practice was for groups of women, aided often by slave seamstresses, to convert cloth issued by the government and cut by experienced tailors into uniforms for entire companies. But as the war continued, provision of clothing became more of an individual enterprise with each family looking after the needs of its own members. During the last two years of the conflict, shortages imposed by the blockade required women to fashion uniforms and other articles of clothing from materials spun and woven at home and colored with homemade dye. Many women became experts in every phase of garment making, and both they and their menfolk took great pride in displaying the results of their handiwork. The great demand for socks caused knitting to become a widespread activity. A South Carolina woman wrote after the war: "We spent all our spare time knitting socks . . . and we never went out to pay a visit without taking our knitting along. It was a common salutation, when we met our firends to say 'Come, bring your knitting and spend the day.' "[17]

Women also helped supplement the meager rations issued to

relatives and friends in the army. Early in the war boxes packed with all sorts of edibles including chicken, ham, cakes, pies, and pickles poured into camps all over the South. This flood dwindled to a trickle in the latter part of the war as transportation facilities deteriorated. The content of boxes was then restricted more and more to simple, durable items such as bread, potatoes, and cured meat.

With increasing economic pressures and the exigencies of war, many women, especially those residing in towns and cities, sought employment in industry and government service. Some worked in ordnance plants making minié balls, paper cartridges, percussion caps, fuses, and shells. Others labored in textile mills and garment factories. Still others performed routine tasks in the Confederate Post Office and Treasury Departments. In the summer of 1864 two hundred women and girls were employed in the Treasury Note Bureau at Columbia, South Carolina, numbering and signing paper currency issued by the government; their performance won the warm praise of the bureau chief, who, of course, was a man. Mary Darby, an aristocratic girl employed in the bureau, found that signing her name nearly three thousand times a day was an onerous chore. She complained that the salary of $250 per month was woefully inadequate when board cost $150 a month and shoes sold for $100 a pair. Later she recalled: ''Those days were some of the saddest yet some of the happiest of my life. When pay-day came, the first time I had ever worked for wages, how mean I felt when I went up and signed for my pay. Rose Wilkinson . . . next to me . . . laughingly said, 'Never mind Mary, I too felt that way at first but you will get beautifully over the feeling and find yourself going up demanding it as your right.' ''[18]

Information on wages of Confederate women who worked in offices and factories is sparse, but the scale apparently was lower than that of men performing the same tasks and was completely out of line with the inflated cost of living.

Teaching, which in antebellum times was done mainly by men or by Yankee "school marms," during the war provided employment for some women. They were usually members of upper class families deprived by Federal invasion of their normal means of support. Some of them deplored being "reduced to teaching" as one of them put it, but adapted well to their changed situation and became good instructors. Others found nothing but unhappiness in trying to dispense knowledge. Among the latter group was Mrs. Edwin H. Fay, a Louisiana aristocrat, who wrote in her diary on July 26, 1863: "Well, my labors as a teacher are over for the present—and I am thankful. . . . Teaching is the most unthankful business on the earth. A great many persons are angry with me . . . because their daughters did not receive honors."[19]

Since the South was predominantly rural, and since most adult white males were in military service, Confederate women had to assume major responsibility for running farms and plantations. Relatively few had the assistance of Negroes, for less than one-fourth of Southern whites in 1860 owned slaves or belonged to slaveholding families. Hence many women, with or without the help of children, had to plant the crops, plow the fields, reap the harvest, kill the hogs, cure the meat, cut the firewood, and perform all the other chores requisite to farming. Moreover, because of restrictions imposed by the blockade, they had to raise food crops, make clothing from materials spun and woven by their labor, tan leather for shoes, and treat illnesses with medicines made at home from roots and herbs gathered from fields and forests. Concerning the experience of Mrs. Aaron Thomas, a North Carolina woman with a large family of small children, a local historian wrote: "There were just not enough daylight hours . . . for her to do all the tasks that must be done and still cultivate her crop. She would get all the children to bed . . . and then go out to the fields to work at night by the light of the moon."[20]

Mrs. Thomas was only one of many impoverished women who

coped successfully with the difficulties created by war. General
Lee cited an instance of remarkable achievement when he wrote
his wife on November 1, 1863:

> I had a visit from a soldier's wife today who was on a visit to
> her husband. She was from Abbeville District S.C. Said she
> had not seen her husband for over two years & as he had
> written to her for clothes she thought she would bring them on
> herself. She brought an entire suit for her husband of her own
> manufacture. She spun the yarn & made the clothes herself.
> She clad her three children in the same way. . . . She was very
> pleasing in her address & modest in her manner . . . an
> admirable woman. Said she was willing to give up everything
> in the world she had to attain our independence. . . . She sat
> with me about ten minutes & took her leave, another mark of
> sense & made no request for herself or husband.[21]

Upper class women who took over the direction of plantations in
some instances displayed outstanding administrative ability.
When R.F.W. Allston of South Carolina died in 1864, his widow
Adele assumed responsibility for running several rice plantations
worked by hundreds of slaves. Her achievements in the face of
formidable difficulty were impressive.[22] Another South Carolina
woman wrote in 1862: "I am a planter for the first time. I insist
upon myself being very energetic and making an appearance of
knowing more than I do."[23] Mrs. Benjamin W. Justice of North
Carolina, with occasional advice written by her officer husband
and with some assistance from relatives and friends, managed a
small plantation for three years with remarkable success. Some
women found the direction of plantations uncongenial and burden-
some. Mrs. W. W. Boyce, wife of a South Carolina congressman,
wrote her husband on April 12, 1862: "I tell [you] candidly all this
attention to farming is uphill work with me. I can give orders first
rate, but when I am not obeyed, I can't keep my temper."[24]

Women of all classes experienced great hardship during the war. The plight of the poor was, of course, worse than that of the privileged; those who suffered most were the impoverished residents of towns and cities. States, counties, municipalities, churches, and philanthropic societies provided some relief, but their efforts fell far short of the need. Hunger caused "bread riots" led by women in Richmond, Augusta, Macon, Petersburg, and other Southern cities.

The women's hardships were increased by marauding Southern soldiers. In November 1863, C. Franklin, a Confederate officer stationed in Columbia County, Arkansas, wrote his congressman: "All here goes wrong. . . . You can hardly believe that men calling themselves Confederate soldiers would be insulting, beating, shooting at & otherwise putting in fear & dread the noble women who have done so much for us, but 'tis even so. It is on every raid Marmaduke or Shelby makes as common as the day. . . . One lady whose husband was in the army & who was herself plowing in the field had her horse in the plow taken from her."[25] Such instances of physical abuse were unusual, but robbery and pillage were widespread. The worst offenders were mounted troops operating in peripheral areas of the South. However, women living in any locality where hungry soldiers were encamped experienced frequent nocturnal raids on their chicken roosts, gardens, and orchards, and the Rebs who made off with the edibles did not trouble themselves to inquire of the owners' loyalties or circumstances. The following complaint, registered by Eliza J. Mountcastle to an unidentified Confederate colonel in July 1862, represented a situation that had many parallels throughout the South: "Col. good Sir will you be so kind as to send a guard to my pig pen the men is so mean they hav taken all of my fowl and talk about takeing my only pig. I never saw such men in my life. . . . I think it is unlawful for ladys to be treated so by a parsel of scamps they are worse than Yankees . . . the[y] have destroyed every thing I hav but my pig."[26]

If Eliza Mountcastle was correct in implying that she received worse treatment from Rebs than from Yanks, her experience was exceptional. As a general rule women living in invaded areas suffered greater hardship than those residing in localities not penetrated by Federal forces. A part of the hardship was the terrible dread with which most women anticipated the coming of the Federals. When Union soldiers approached Southern communities, whether in northern Virginia in 1861, Middle Tennessee in 1862, north Georgia in 1864, or South Carolina in 1865, women spent sleepless nights and anxious days hiding valuables, saying prayers, and building up their courage for reception of the "wicked Vandals" descending upon them. Often the anticipation of invasion was worse than the reality, for most Northern generals tried to prevent their men from entering private homes or personally abusing helpless civilians. Even so, restraining orders frequently were ignored. Captain Charles Wills of an Illinois regiment wrote from near Oxford, Mississippi, in December 1862: "Rebels though they are, 'tis shocking and enough to make one's blood boil to see the manner in which some of our folks have treated them. Trunks have been knocked to pieces with muskets when the women stood by, offering the keys . . . bed clothing and ladies' clothing carried off and all manner of deviltry imaginable perpetrated. Of course the scoundrels who do this kind of work would be severely punished if caught, but the latter is almost impossible. Most of the mischief is done by the advance of the army. . . . the d——d thieves even steal from the Negroes!"[27] A Wisconsin corporal wrote at the conclusion of Sherman's "March to the Sea" in December 1864: "The cruelties practiced on the campaign toward citizens have been enough to blot a more sacred cause than ours. We hardly deserve success. . . . Straggler's under nobody's charge . . . ransack the houses, taking every knife and fork, spoon, or anything else they take a fancy to, break open trunks and bureaus, taking women or children's clothing, or tearing them to pieces . . . besides taking everything eatable that can be found. . . . there is certainly a lack of discipline in our army.''[28]

Sherman's forces were even more destructive in South Carolina than in Georgia because of the widespread feeling that South Carolinians deserved special punishment for initiating secession. A Pennsylvania soldier wrote in his memoirs: ''When we reached the South Carolina side of the river, General Geary roade along the marching column and said 'Boys are you well supplied with matches as we are now in South Carolina.' It was not necessary for the General to remind the boys of this fact.''[29] Another soldier wrote just after completing the march through South Carolina: ''We burnt every house, barn, mill that we passed. . . . We took just what we wanted, cry or no cry. . . . Everybody knows and I know that South Carolina has needed a good whipping and she has got it right and left.''[30] An Illinois preacher-soldier wrote in his diary while in Charleston, South Carolina, in April 1865: ''Many of our Boys will push into houses where only women are the inmates and Steal and Rob all the[y] Can Lay there unholy hands on and often treat the women Rudely.''[31] Rape was rare, but it did occur.[32]

Many women elected to flee with their families rather than risk the perils of invasion. These displaced persons frequently experienced greater hardship than those who stayed at home. Travel was difficult and expensive. Sometimes the migrants had to move more than once to keep out of the path of invasion. Opportunities for remunerative employment were limited, and the presence of refugees created problems in the communities where they settled. Prices rose, streets were crowded, and disease increased. It is not surprising that refugees sometimes encountered hostility from regular residents when they sought to establish new homes in strange localities. Most of them suffered from loneliness, homesickness, boredom, and a feeling of insecurity. One of them wrote in her diary: ''There is nothing to mark one day from another now—always the same, sew, knit, read. . . . Oh I get so tired of it.''[33] Another wrote: ''My heart feels often as if it would break

with longing for home."[34] But some refugees learned to laugh at
their troubles and a few seemed to enjoy life in their new homes.
Among the latter group was Kate Stone who fled from Louisiana to
Texas with her mother, but Kate was young, pretty, and bouyant
and had enough means to assure a sufficiency of food and clothing.
Women who stayed at home to confront the invaders reacted in
various ways. Some greeted the Federals cordially, either because
of genuine Unionist leanings or because they hoped to obtain
favors. Most of them, however, bore too deep a hatred for the men
in blue to make any pretense of friendliness. Nannie Haskins, a
teenager of Clarksville, Tennessee, wrote in her diary early in
1863: "[I] never see [a Yankee] but what I roll my eyes, grit my
teeth, and almost shake my fist at him, and then bite my lip . . . and
turn away in disgust."[35] A young lady of Fredericksburg, Virginia, wrote to a friend in May 1863, after the Federals retreated
through the town following their disastrous defeat at Chancellorsville: "My only amusement was watching them bury their dead. I
got quite fond of looking at [the corpses]. . . . Horrible wretches! I
pray they may never return."[36] In January 1862 an Indiana soldier
wrote from Pilot Knob, Tennessee: "I have been to almost every
farm house within five miles. . . . Everyone I meet are secessionist
. . . the *women* have denounced me most bitterly."[37] In New
Orleans and other Southern cities occupied by the Federals,
women cursed the men in blue, cheered for Jeff Davis, pretended
to be nauseated when encountering Union soldiers on the streets,
or stepped off the sidewalks to avoid proximity with them or with
the Union flag. Some women doused the Federals with dishwater
or with the contents of chamberpots. Major Abner Small of the
Sixteenth Maine Regiment wrote in his diary in July 1864, after
being marched with other Union prisoners through the streets of
Petersburg: "The sidewalks were lined with old men, boys, and
decrepit women who vied with one another in flinging insults and
venom. The women were the worst of the lot; they spat upon us,
laughed at us and called us vile and filthy names."[38] A Mas-

sachusetts colonel in his official report of operations at Winchester, Virginia, wrote on May 25, 1862: "My retreating column suffered serious loss in the streets. . . . Males and females vied with each other in increasing the number of their victims by firing from the houses, throwing hand grenades, hot water, and missiles of every description."[39]

The verbal retaliation to which openly defiant Rebel women were sometimes subjected is vividly illustrated by the report that Private William H. Parkinson of Illinois gave to his homefolk after his regiment encountered a fiery feminine patriot in West Tennessee in July 1862:

As we came out . . . from Jackson, we met quite a nice young Lady, with a young Gent riding by her side. Nevins (Col.) spoke to her very polite & she Hurrahed for Jeff Davis. He paid no attention to it. As she passed on the boys Spoke very polite to her, raising their hats, but she answered in the Same way. As She was passing a Sergeant in the rear of the Reg. he was just in the act of raising his hat to her, when *She belched out* "Hurrah for Jeff Davis." He did not raise his hat but Said, "By G—d, Maddam, *your Cunt* is all that Saves your life" & I do know She was the maddest Girl I Ever Saw, but She did not Say another word.[40]

Antipathy sometimes tended to lessen as Northern units tarried in occupied communities and as personal acquaintances developed between the invaders and invaded. Colonel Hans C. Heg wrote his wife in Murfreesboro in May 1863: "The people living around here are not as strong secesh as they used to be, in fact I am pretty sure many of the young ladies would be right glad to marry some of our gay and handsome looking officers."[41] Some Tennessee women did marry Yankee soldiers and the same can be said of those of every other Confederate state. Colonel Heg told of one of his men marrying a West Tennessee woman whose first husband was a Rebel soldier but who, in her words, was "supposed to be dead."[42]

Confederate women who fraternized with their foes were rarely, if ever, more than a small minority of occupied communities. Continuing contact with the Federals often intensified the hatred of many women. The Federal presence was both an instrument and a reminder of the hardships and deprivations born of war; as it persisted and spread, it signified an increasing likelihood of Southern defeat and the overthrow of slavery. A Georgia woman noted in her journal on December 20, 1863: "Our prospects seem rather gloomy at present. I do not fear subjugation . . . but I fear the Negro. I tremble for the institution of slavery; it is well nigh done for."[43] A low country South Carolinian wrote in her diary during Federal invasion in February 1865: "What I most fear is not the Yankees but the Negroes. . . . What will become of us? . . . Disorder has already started."[44]

One of the greatest hardships experienced by Confederate women was anxiety about loved ones serving in the armed forces. In July 1863, a Texas woman wrote to her sister: "I am nearly crazy about my old man," and the next year a South Carolina lawyer wrote his friend, James H. Hammond: "My wife, strong & active, full of energy, with the will to accomplish all she desires, is showing failing symptoms. Her only two boys are in the field . . . on their way to Virginia. She would not have them stay, & yet in the still watches of the night I can hear her deep sighs & sometimes suppressed moans, I know she is thinking of them."[45] Many Confederate women had numerous loved ones about whom to worry, for families normally were large. The combined effects of zeal for volunteering in the early months of the conflict and the compulsion of the draft during the last three years had swept most adult males and many boys into military service. The fact that a white population of about five and one-half million Southerners provided armed forces of about one million men meant that families who sent no one to war were rare and that those who provided several were not uncommon. Mrs. B. G. Bledsoe of Newton County, Mississippi, gave ten sons and five sons-in-law to Confederate military service; Mrs. Enoch Hooper Cook of Alabama gave a husband, ten sons, and two grandsons; Flora Macdonald Jones and Lucy Faucett Simpson of North Carolina gave eleven sons each. Scores of other women contributed from five to ten sons.[46]

Confederate women had good cause to be anxious about the men they sent to war. Battles were extraordinarily destructive because troops marched in mass formation against deadly weapons, and provisions for the care of the wounded were woefully inadequate. But disease was the great killer in the Civil War, causing more than twice as many deaths as did hostile bullets. On the Confederate side, estimated deaths from all causes totaled 258,000; on the average, then, more than one out of every four men who donned the gray failed to survive the conflict and, of those who did, many were partially or totally incapacitated by wounds or sickness.

Some Confederate women bore a disproportionate share of the war's heavy toll in human lives. Mrs. Polly Ray, a Tar Heel widow, lost all seven sons in the war, and a neighbor, Mrs. Charity Boyles, lost six of seven sons; another North Carolinian, Mrs. Oran Palmer, had four sons killed at Gettysburg; and Mrs. John Banks of Georgia lost three of her nine soldier sons in the Atlanta campaign.[47] Anne F. Scott, in *The Southern Lady: From Pedestal to Politics, 1830-1930*, cites the remarkable instance of one mother who lost nine of the twelve sons whom she sent to war.[48]

Most women who lost loved ones were far removed from the scene of tragedy. It is not surprising then that some did not learn of their loss until long after it occurred. An exception was an instance involving Mrs. William Mason Smith, a widow of South Carolina, whose son Willie was seriously wounded at Cold Harbor near Richmond on June 3, 1864. Mrs. Smith went to Virginia to look after her son, and was almost constantly at his bedside during the six weeks that he lingered. Her anguish was vividly portrayed in

her letters. On August 12, 1864, she wrote her brother: "Dear
Pringle, my boy is dying, slowly, but surely . . . perhaps a few
hours may bring rest for his tortured body, & I *believe* safety for
his soul. . . . Motion is torture. He is drugged with Morphine all the
time yet feels the pain; wakes up screaming. Chloroform exhausts
him so it cannot be much used. . . . You can understand how I feel
when I tell you that when it is quietly over I shall say 'thank
God.' " Willie died four days later and the widow, who the year
before had lost her twelve-year-old son from diphtheria, returned
home to share her grief with her daughters. But her days of anxiety
were not over for two younger sons in their late teens were still in
the army. Fortunately they survived unharmed. [49]

Many Confederate women were sustained in their enormous
suffering by a firm reliance on Divine Providence. One woman
wrote her soldier son in December 1864: "What would I do
without the promises of God to them that trust in him?" [50] A
Georgian told her sister after the loss of a brother at Fredericksburg: "Alas, dark would be our despair if we could not say 'It is the
Lord who hath done what seemeth to him right.' " [51]

During the early part of the conflict Southern women manifested
an increase of religious interest by attending church in greater
numbers and participating more actively in religious programs.
But their zeal began to decline after a while and during the last two
years of the war ministers often complained about shrinking con-
gregations and the waning of interest in spiritual activities. The
decline in church attendance was partly the result of the difficulty
of obtaining decent clothing and the shortage of horses and vehi-
cles on which many people depended for conveyance to religious
services. Undoubtedly other influences contributed to spiritual
lethargy, among them the failure of the South to win the quick
victory that ministers and other leaders had promised and the
increasing burden of hardship that came with prolongation of the
conflict. [52]

As religion declined immorality increased. [53] A Confederate

Mrs. Phoebe Yates Pember, Chief Matron, 1862-1865, Division No. 2, Chimborazo Hospital, Richmond, Virginia

Painting by Malcolm Thurgood, from a Civil War photograph. Courtesy of McCowat-Mercer Press

Georgia Confederate women on a visit to their husbands in a camp near Richmond, Virginia, early in 1862. Officer standing at extreme right, holding his wife's hand, is Lt. Col. Thos. C. Johnson, who was killed on June 26, 1862, while leading the 19th Ga. Reg't. in the Battle of Mechanicsville.

Mississippian widowed by the war. Mrs. Bettie Gill, whose husband, Lt. Robert M. Gill, was killed at the Battle of Jonesboro, Georgia, August 31, 1864.

Courtesy of Jean S. A. Brasfield, Columbus, Mississippi

Rebecca White Barfield of Yazoo County, Mississippi, who in 1865 married Lt. Robert J. McCormack, of 3d Miss. Reg't.

Courtesy of Mrs. H. E. McCormack, Carthage, Mississippi

Captain Sally L. Tompkins, founder and head of military hospital, Richmond, Virginia. Only Confederate woman to hold a military commission.

major stationed near Knoxville wrote his wife in June 1863: "I will state as a matter of history that female virtue if it ever existed in this Country seems now almost a perfect wreck. Prostitutes are thickly crowded through mountain & valley in hamlet & city."[54] Six months later a captain encamped near Chattanooga wrote in his diary: "The war appears to have demoralized everybody and the rumor says that almost half the women in the vicinity of the army, married and unmarried, are lost to all virtue."[55]

Deterioration of morals was by no means confined to East Tennessee. A cavalry captain stationed in North Mississippi wrote his wife in March 1864 that women were involved in illicit trading in cotton with Federals in Memphis. He added: "In N.E. Miss there are numerous cases of illegitimacy among the wives too of soldiers who have been gallantly fighting in Virginia for two years."[56] In October 1864, a Confederate private, encamped near Pollard, Alabama, wrote his wife: "We are in the poorest pine country you ever saw, the people can raise nothing but potatoes. The state of morals is quite low as the soil. Almost all the women are given to whoredom & [they are] the ugliest, tallow faced, shaggy headed, bare footed, dirty wenches you ever saw."[57]

Prostitution flourished in the cities, especially in the Confederate capital. In August 1864, the mayor of that city stated: "Never was a place more changed than Richmond. Go on the Capitol Square any afternoon and you may see the women promenading up & down the shady walks jostling respectable ladies into the gutter . . . [or] leaning upon the arms of Confederate officers."[58] Hunger was a factor contributing to prostitution. A Confederate officer who made an inspection of the Army of Tennessee at Dalton, Georgia, in April 1864, reported that "lewd women" were "impregnating this whole command" and that the commissariat had been "frequently robbed with a view of supporting these disreputable characters."[59] In invaded areas needy women were sometimes pressured into prostitution by the offer of Federal provisions. In September 1864 a Confederate woman living near Atlanta wrote her husband that she had been approached by Union soldiers who told her "if I wod comedate them I never shold suffe[r] for . . . the[y] wod [fe[tc]h me anything to eat I wanted." She told the soldiers that she was an "onis woman" and would "see them burnt alive" before she would yield to their lust. But she informed her husband that several married neighbors, whom she named, were "horin" with the Federals in exchange for flour, meal, meat, sugar, crackers, and coffee.[60]

Of course, wrong doing was not universal among Confederate women in invaded areas or anywhere else. But there can be no doubt that the war caused a deterioration of morals and that immorality was much more common in 1865 than in 1861.

The activities and attitudes of the Confederacy's Negro women are very difficult to determine because of the scarcity of pertinent records. Very few of the black women could write, so an estimate of what they thought and did has to be formed from a study of the records kept by whites. These records indicate that in the uninvaded areas of the South, life of the slave women was little affected by the war. But in regions penetrated by the Federals great changes occurred. Many house servants remained loyal to their owners because of their privileged position in the slave hierarchy and their long, relatively intimate association with the whites. But loyalty of the house servants was by no means universal. In a number of instances Negro women who helped their mistresses hide silver and other valuables on the approach of the invaders later revealed the location of the treasure to the Federals.[61]

Slave women who worked in the fields—and they were far more numerous than the house servants—along with their men folk and their children ran away in large numbers when the Federals came close enough to make their escape feasible. Whether they ran away to hasten the breaking of their bonds or waited until the Federals brought emancipation to them, the overwhelming majority of slaves greeted the invaders with great joy and seized freedom with obvious alacrity. On May 16, 1862, shortly after the Federals reached the vicinity of Fredericksburg, Virginia, Mrs. Betty Herndon Maury of that town wrote in her diary: "Matters are getting worse and worse here every day with regard to the negroes. They are leaving their owners by the hundreds and demanding wages."[62] General W. T. Sherman stated that when his forces on the march to the sea entered Covington, Georgia, with bands playing and flags flying, "The Negroes were simply frantic with joy. Whenever they heard my name, they clustered about my horse, shouted and prayed." He added: "I have witnessed hundreds if not thousands of such scenes; and can see now a poor girl in the very ecstasy of the Methodist 'shout', hugging the banner of one of the regiments and jumping up to the 'feet of Jesus.' "[63]

Countless other incidents throughout the South evidenced the slaves' yearning for freedom. On the Sunday afternoon of the battle of First Bull Run, a Negro cook was preparing Sunday dinner for her master and his family in a kitchen detached from the plantation house. Occasionally she could hear the firing of the cannon on the distant battlefield. Each time she heard the rumbling of the guns she cried out in a voice loud enough for fellow slaves in the yard to hear her: "Ride on Massa Jesus, ride on!"[64] Many of the ex-slaves interviewed by Works Progress Administration investigators in the 1930s recalled attending nightly prayer meetings during the Civil War and praying fervently for Union victory and freedom.[65] Old folks' recollections of events so far removed frequently are unreliable, but there is no reason for doubting the testimony of venerable blacks throughout the South that during the conflict involving emancipation they prayed surreptitiously and earnestly for the emancipators. Minnie Davis, for example, was credible when she recalled that during her girlhood in Confederate Georgia, while her master was praying aloud that the Lord would drive the Yankees back, her mother was silently praying "Oh Lord, please send the Yankees on and let them set us free."[66]

Freedom was sometimes disillusioning, especially to the Negro women. Federal soldiers in some instances ransacked slave cabins, took the occupants' belongings, and abused, insulted, and even raped the black women. Early in May 1863, a Confederate captain who owned a plantation near Vicksburg wrote: "They [Yankees] are worse than the Goths and Vandals of the middle ages. . . . All the Negro women were ravished, the Yanks holding them whilst others were gratifying their hellish desires. This is the testimony of the old Negroes."[67] Federal sources indicate that some maltreatment of Negro women by Union soldiers occurred throughout the invaded South. On January 10, 1865, General O. O. Howard, then at Beaufort, South Carolina, wrote one of his corps commanders: "General, I feel surprised . . . to find that many depredations have been committed near this place, and certain things done that would disgrace us even in the enemy's country, *e.g.* the robbing of some negroes and abusing their women."[68]

In view of the demoralizing influences of war and the fact that many Northern soldiers were racists, it is not surprising that Negroes suffered some abuse at their hands. But with all its shortcomings the blacks still preferred freedom to the bondage they had known before the Yankees came. In some instances wholesome relationships developed between black women and white Yankees. Richard H. Mockett, a Milwaukee shoemaker of the Forty-third Michigan Regiment, wrote in his diary at Nashville, January 1, 1865: "I met one of the kindest old colored ladies in this city I ever saw. She was as good to me as a mother. She got me up splendid meals and attended to my comfort as if I was her own son. . . . I paid the old man and woman well and shall never forget them. The old ladies name was Barbara Allen; she wished me to remember it."[69]

While the Negroes were fraternizing with their emancipators the Confederacy's white women sought to alleviate their loneliness and anxiety. In the cities those who had the leisure and the means attended theaters, where musicals, comedies, and tragedies were played by professionals. Dinner parties, picnics, barbecues, molasses candy pullings, and dances were popular in both town and country. Young people especially liked to get together for what they called "singing sprees"; favorite songs included "Lorena," "Annie Laurie," "Juanita," "Dixie," "The Girl I Left Behind Me," "All Quiet Along the Potomac Tonight," "Just Before the Battle Mother," and "Home Sweet Home."

In July 1864 a rural Georgia girl wrote to her aunt: "Dull times down here. You never saw such a scarcity of men in your life. . . . I wish this ugly war would close. . . . Widowers and Shinplasters is about played out; they all have to skedaddle to the war."[70] Shortage of males was a common complaint among Confederate women of courting age, and put additional responsibility on boys who were not old enough for military service. Some of them registered jocular protest. One teenage lad wrote his bachelor uncle in the army: "I am still flying around with the girls. . . . I went to meting . . . at Union and coming home I had to keep company with about a dozen girls. . . . I want you to make haste . . . and come home to help me out for I tell you that I have my hands full."[71]

Women living near army camps sometimes attended reviews, band concerts, theatricals, and parties given by military personnel. The arrival of a military unit in a community always enlivened social activity. Twenty-year-old Lezinka White of Yazoo City, Mississippi, wrote a friend on March 3, 1865: "We have a party occasionally whenever any soldiers come to town, and we enjoy it very much, because it is so rarely we have a chance to dance. Just before Lent there were five or six parties in town, because Gen'l. Ross brigade of Texas soldiers (who are great favorites in this place) had returned from their hard and disasterous campaign in Tennessee."[72]

Women of all ages and classes got together from time to time to spin, weave, sew, or just talk. The standard refreshment for such occasions was "Confederate" coffee made of parched particles of sweet potatoes, corn, or English peas with sorghum added to provide "long sweetening." If pastries were served, they usually differed from prewar desserts in that they were sweetened with molasses, honey, or a sirup made from watermelon juice. The most common topic of conversation was "the war," particularly the activities and prospects of sons, brothers, husbands, and sweethearts. Another frequently discussed topic, of course, was children, especially their health, growth, and schooling. Education was complicated by a shortage of teachers and textbooks. Many mothers assumed responsibility for teaching their own children, but this was sometimes an impossible task because of the heavy demands of other household duties. Virginia French of McMinnville, Tennessee, wrote in her diary on May 26, 1862: "I have the children with me constantly . . . from morning till night. I have commenced teaching them to write. Reading, spelling, writing, notation, speeches, drawing and music occupy a large portion of our time. I must endeavor to do them justice, if everything else should be left by the board."[73] The typical elementary school during the war was a subscription institution, with one teacher serving the children of several families. Schools reflected the martial spirit in various ways. Textbooks, prepared especially for Southern children, posed such problems as "If one confederate soldier kill 90 yankees, how many yankees can 10 confederate soldiers kill?" or, *Question*: "What is the present drawback in our trade?" *Answer*: "An unlawful Blockade by the miserable and hellish Yankee nation."[74] At Scotch Cross Academy, a subscription school in South Carolina, the pupils "caught the spirit of patriotism from their parents and spent the hours during recess knitting socks and suspenders for the soldiers."[75] All schools felt the pinch of war. Many of them permitted students to pay part or all of their expenses in corn, wheat, meat, or other farm products. In boarding schools food became scarcer and less palatable. One of the pupils at Madame Togno's school for girls, which moved from Charleston to Barhamville, South Carolina, during the war, wrote afterward: "Tea and coffee had to be left out and one thing after another, until we ceased to come into the dining-room at all for supper. Two large trays of very dry corn-dodgers were brought into the school room at tea-time, accompanied by two large pitchers of water and a tray of glasses.''[76] Some boarding schools were converted into coeducational institutions during the war, which sometimes created problems. A girl who attended one of the new-type schools in Texas wrote a friend: ''Plenty of the Louisiana refugees who think themselves a grade above Texians are attending our school; the little boys and girls from 12 to 15 years old are taking the day, they consider themselves *grown*, they walk [together] and write love letters at an extensive rate, I have no doubt but that some of them are engaged.''[77]

Still another topic of conversation at the women's get-togethers was clothing, especially fashions. Older women explained and sometimes demonstrated to younger ones procedures for carding, spinning, and weaving; for making dye from homegrown indigo, walnut hulls, and the roots, bark, or leaves of various vines, shrubs, and trees; and for setting or fixing the color with copperas obtained by soaking metal in a kettle of water. Old and young exchanged information about making homespun materials into blouses, coats, and skirts, and about converting cloth, palmetto leaves, and wheat straw into bonnets or hats, and trimming the headpieces with lace, ribbon, feathers, flowers, berries, or leaves. Women took justifiable pride in their skills in converting old garments into new ones by re-dying material, using it in different combinations, or changing the style. Hoops were discarded by some, but upper class women tended to cling to the billowing skirts for dress occasions; they also made relatively little use of homespun, depending instead on re-made finery of prewar times or on new clothing obtained from outside the South. A young Georgia aristocrat wrote one of her friends in March 1863: ''I am going into the [Federal] lines . . . and expect to get the prettiest wardrobe which Paris or France afford. . . . I am so delighted, for really I have not felt lady like for the past two years, my wardrobe has been in such a dilapidated condition.''[78] That other and older women longed for finery, now made impossible by the blockade, is indicated by a letter of Mrs. James G. Ramsay of North Carolina to her husband, a member of the Confederate Senate, November 18, 1864: ''Maj. Kinders says they have Godey and harpers in the [congressional] reading rooms. I wish you would get some and send me for I want to see the fashions.''[79] If Mrs. Ramsay's request was fulfilled, she, being a generous woman, must have shared the magazines with her Rowan County friends when they got together for Confederate cookies and tea.

Women traveled more during the war than before, mainly to visit relatives or friends in military service. Long trips were usually made by train, which were crowded, slow, dirty, and uncomfortable. Train wrecks were frequent because of excessive traffic, poor rails, defective equipment, and inefficient operation. The danger and discomfort of travel apparently was no deterrent to women who had the money, the time, and the inclination to be near loved ones in the army. During the war, much more than before, women moved from place to place without male escort.

For the privileged few who had leisure and materials, reading was a favorite diversion. Many lower class women were illiterate, and those who weren't frequently were so absorbed in taking care of their families that they had neither the time nor the energy for reading. The Bible was the most widely read of all books; newspapers were in great demand because of the general eagerness for information about the progress of the war and the activities of relatives and friends in military service.

The journal of Catherine Edmonston, wife of a North Carolina officer-planter, affords an insight into the reading tastes and habits of an upper class Confederate woman. Mrs. Edmonston was childless, had access to a good library, and enjoyed abundant leisure. Her reading extended to a diversity of books, including the works of Milton, Spenser, Byron, Coleridge, Burns, Gibbon, Macaulay, Motley, Bacon, and Bulwer-Lytton. She had a special

interest in military history. During the war she kept herself well
informed about battles and leaders through a careful reading of
newspapers. On September 11, 1862, she wrote: "I am trying to
read . . . the first part of *Les Miserables*, but it is uphill work
—coarse, radical & unprincipled. . . . I fear vulgarity revolts me
more than wickedness." On January 9, 1865, she noted: "I have
been reading Motley's *United Netherlands* & have derived great
comfort from it. We are not so divided, lean not so much on
foreign aid & are not reduced near so low as they were, & yet by
perseverance they triumphed."[80] The journal of another aristocratic lady, young Kate Stone of Louisiana, contains references to
more than thirty authors, among them Shakespeare, Bulwer-
Lytton, Hugo, Lamb, Hawthorne, Tennyson, and Thackery. On
February 1, 1862, she wrote: "Have nothing new to read. Thus I
have taken my old favorite, Scott, the Prince of Novelists. Who of
modern writers can compare with him?"[81]

   On May 30, 1862, Ella Harper of Lenoir, North Carolina, wrote
her soldier husband: "I never liked to write letters before, but it is a
pleasure as well as a relief now."[82] For Mrs. Harper, as for
innumerable other Confederate women, corresponding with loved
ones in the army provided frequent and highly cherished diversion;
and in what they wrote they revealed very much about themselves.
In the letters of married women the most striking attribute is the
deep affection of wives for their husbands. Such devotion was not,
of course, universal. Separation made the women more keenly
aware of affection for their husbands and of the deepening of their
love with the passing of time. In some instances wives were timid
about giving expression to their affection—even to the extent of
addressing their spouses as "My dear friend." But their reserve
usually lessened as they became accustomed to correspondence.

   Mrs. Ella Harper wrote her husband on July 15, 1862: "Sometimes when I am writing to you my heart gets so full of love that if I
was to follow its dictation, I fear you would think my letter very
lovesick and foolish." Three months later she informed him: "I

have about finished your drawers. I love to sew for you. I have such sweet, loving thoughts about you. If your body is as warm when wearing the clothes as my heart is while making them, you will be very comfortable."[83]

Mrs. George W. Peddy and her husband, who was surgeon of the Fifty-sixth Georgia Regiment, seemed to try to outdo each other in avowing their affection. On December 19, 1861, she wrote in response to one of her spouse's sugary missives: "My best beloved. . . . I often wonder whether every woman loved like me; I know they can't for one of the many reasons—they do not have . . . one of nature's noblemen as I am blest with on which to bestow their love." Three months later she wrote: "I know you love me Honey, but I am so childish as to love for you to be continually telling me so." The Peddy correspondence remained highly romantic throughout the war.[84]

The letters of wives to their husbands did not generally allude to the physical aspects of love. But reading between the lines clearly suggests that marital relationships of the 1860s were little different from those of today. A Confederate wife who addressed her husband as "Sweetest, Precious, Darling, Charming Billy" wrote him in 1864: "Honey . . . I so much dislike this way we are living, you way in one part of the world and me in another . . . Sometimes I think I am doing very well and then again I get to studying about you and I take the all overs, get in a perfect Fever. . . . I have got a spell this evening I feel like I would give a world of Confederacys just to be with you."[85] On April 22, 1864, a South Carolina woman wrote her husband: "My loving John I feel like I would squees and huge you to death if I had the chance. You should not sleep in a weeak when I got my arms around you. I will make up for loss time; so you may hold yourself in rediness."[86] Fear of pregnancy was a source of considerable concern.[87] Some wives prolonged the nursing period of infants because of a widespread belief that lactation was a deterrent to conception. Reunions, however eagerly anticipated, were nearly always followed by periods of anxiety. Brigadier General Dorsey Pender wrote his wife after one of her visits in 1862: "My mind was very much relieved to hear that you were not as I had imagined. . . . If you do not want children, you will have to remain away from me, and hereafter when you come to me I shall know that you want another baby."[88]

Many wives of officers showed great interest in their husbands' promotion. Mrs. Braxton Bragg affords a good example of the "pushy" wife. On October 13, 1861 she wrote her husband: "*Mansfield Lovell*, never conspicuous that I am aware of . . . has been raised to the same rank as yourself. . . . Surely, surely you will not submit to this." A month before Shiloh she stated: "I have lost the little confidence I ever had in the President's favorite S. Johnson, & he *ranks you*. Beauregard is an egotist, Polk a wild enthusiast, & both *rank* you. . . . How I wish, dear husband, that you could be [the army commander], not for the gratification of any personal vanity, but because I truly feel, & the President *knows* . . . you are the only one capable of managing volunteers."[89] Despite Bragg's subsequent failures as an army commander, Mrs. Bragg clung to the view that he was not accorded the recognition he deserved.

Mrs. Bragg evidenced another quality frequently found among Confederate women, namely, strong views on military policy and public affairs, along with a readiness to express these views to family and friends. These opinions often were sound. In October 1862, shortly after the battle of Perryville, Mrs. Bragg wrote her husband: "You have, it is true, made a very rapid march but without defeating your wary foe. . . . It will be very hard for you to have to assume the defensive, & to have to fall back when so much was expected from your army. . . . I hoped you would have cleared Tennessee as you advanced."[90] After Chickamauga she wrote: "I fear our victory is like all we are ever permitted to gain, *undecisive* & with a fearful loss of men. . . . Rosecrans still holds the points *he* aimed at—Chattanooga, East Tennessee, Cumberland Gap."[91] Such perceptive observations make one wonder if Elsie Bragg, rather than Braxton, should not have worn the general's stars.

Augusta Evans Wilson, the Mobile novelist, was another woman who expressed herself freely on military and political matters—not to her husband, for she was unmarried—but to General Beauregard whom she greatly admired and to Congressman J. L. M. Curry of Alabama. She criticized Jefferson Davis for lack of aggressiveness after First Manassas, condemned making ownership of slaves a basis for exemption from military service, compared Stonewall Jackson's achievements with those of Gustavus Adolphus, and through her published writings served as propagandist for the Southern cause. She also deplored the Confederacy's failure to make fuller use of the talents of women in its bid for independence.[92]

Mary Ann Cobb, wife of the Confederate congressman and general, Howell Cobb, also was outspoken on public issues and Confederate leaders. In her letters to her husband two of her favorite targets were Governor Joseph Brown of Georgia, whom she loathed, and Vice-President Alexander Stephens. Concerning a minor incident involving the equipping of Cobb's Legion, commanded by her brother-in-law, she wrote: "I have not been so excited not to say mad for some time. I believe really it was a snare of the devil to entrap me into speaking unadvisedly with my lips. I did so considerably, Brown, Stephens & Toombs as my topics." After the famous peace talks at Hampton's Roads in February 1865, she wrote: "*Paul* went to the good *Ananias* to receive his sight again—but Stephens had to go to Lincoln & Seward."[93]

Wives of Confederate congressmen sometimes offered opinions concerning pending legislation. Mrs. James G. Ramsay took a strong position against putting Negroes into Confederate ranks. "If you ever vote to arm the Negroes," she wrote in November 1864, "you need not come home."[94]

Mrs. Ramsay was no "clinging vine" and the same may be said of many other Confederate women, who spoke their views and who were listened to with respect by their husbands. Most women were very tactful when giving advice on matters not purely domestic. Mrs. John C. Breckinridge in offering a suggestion concerning the staff of her husband, the general, stated: "I have no right to say anything except privately, and as you advocate free speech I may venture to express an opinion."[95] Wives who were compelled by the fortunes of war to take over the direction of farms and plantations usually were very careful to seek their husbands' counsel concerning details of management. The men were undoubtedly pleased by the deference to their judgment, but often their response was in effect: do what you think is best. Some expressed appreciation of the women's achievements; among them was a Georgia lieutenant who wrote his wife in 1862: "You will get to be such a managing business body by the time I get back that I have made up my mind to give up everything & bow in meek humility to petticoat government & submit quietly to your tyrannical rule, curtain lectures included."[96] A Georgia private in 1863 informed his wife: "I cannot pass over without letting you [know] how well pleased [I am] with your management of . . . affairs. I have almost come to the conclusion that if you have good luck . . . you would get rich."[97]

In their letters to relatives and friends, some women demonstrated a humor so earthy as to contradict the romantic tradition of universal refinement among Southern ladies of the hoopskirt era. A Confederate lieutenant who wrote teasingly to his wife about possible impotence from a recent bout with the mumps received a reply so racy as to evoke the comment: "Mollie, I read a part of your letter to the boys and we had a great laf about . . . the mumps not having hurt me. I did not let them see all of it." When he playfully rebuked his wife for presenting him another daughter instead of a son he got the spicy retort: "I think you give your boys to some one else.''[98] A Georgia girl, obviously not a "poor white," wrote in 1864 to her friend, Mollie:

> We young ladies had a very nice time [canoeing with the boys] . . . on the river. . . . One of the girls caught an eel; it frightened her so bad she thundered from below. . . . I laugh until I thought I never would get home. . . . A few days before that we went fishing and one of the girls fell over the fence and showed her you know what; it look like a new moon. You never saw boys skedaddle so in your life. . . . You said something about my shitting scrapes. . . . Of all the shitting . . . ever known, the people of Jones [County] can't be beat; ever body is sick; ask them what's the matter, "got the shits". . . . A person [would] as soon as be dead as to be out of the fashion, therefore I follow suit.[99]

The correspondence of Confederate women also illustrates their staunchness in adversity. A good case in point is that of Mrs. Margaret McCalla of Morristown, Tennessee, who, on the approach of the Federals in September 1863, took her aged mother, three small children, several slaves, and two wagon loads of household goods two hundred miles over rough country into South Carolina. There she bought a farm, buried one son, gave birth to another, and maintained herself and her dependents until the end of the war. The letters she wrote to her husband during the long, trying exile reveal a woman of great sturdiness, resourcefulness, and character. She kept her husband fully informed of her activities, but tried always to avoid causing him undue concern about his family. On June 6, 1864, she wrote that her desire to see him was almost unbearable, but added: "Knowing that nothing but imperative duty keeps you away, I wrestle with yearning for your society constantly so as to keep it in bounds and not intrude it upon you thereby causing you to feel more anxious about me."[100]

The same sort of consideration was shown by other wives. Mrs. J. B. Jett, who sustained herself and several children by running a farm near Atlanta, wrote her soldier husband, as the Federals approached her neighborhood in June 1864: ''I don't know what to doo. I haint got the money to take us of[f], so we will hafter [have to] stand the test. . . . Don't be on easy about me. I intend to doo the best I can.'' The invaders ransacked her house, killed her hogs, and took all her corn and wheat. Somehow she managed to eke out a living until the end of the war.[101] Comparable to Mrs. Jett in resourcefulness and stamina was a Virginia woman who late in the war, while struggling mightily to provide for herself and her children, wrote her husband: ''Donte be uneasy about ous. We will try and take care of [our]selves thebest we can. I donte minde what I have to do [just] so you can get backe safe.''[102]

No class of Confederate women possessed greater capacity for endurance than the yeomanry. Yet many of this class were broken in spirit by the enormous hardships they were subjected to in the latter part of the war. Deprived of their menfolk by a draft that allowed no exemption for dependents, and victimized by inflation, speculation, and hoarding, they poured out their woes in pitiful letters to state governors and other officials. Governor Zebulon Vance of North Carolina, largely because he was thought to have a sincere interest in the welfare of the masses, was the recipient of an exceptionally large number of these letters. In January 1865, one who signed herself ''A Poor Woman and Children,'' wrote Vance: ''For the sake of suffering humanity . . . and especially for the sake of sufering women and children try and stop this cruel war, here I am without one mouthful to eat for myself and five children and God only knows where I will get som thing now you know as well as you have a head that it is impossible to whip the Yankees . . . my husband has been kiled, and if they all stay till they are dead what in they name of God will become of us poor women.''[103]

Even more poignant must have been the letters that the poor

women sent to their husbands. Unfortunately, few of them have been preserved. One that was kept (because it was presented as evidence at a court-martial) stated:

> My dear Edward:—I have always been proud of you, and since your connection with the Confederate army, I have been prouder of you than ever before. I would not have you do anything wrong for the world, but before God, Edward, unless you come home we must die. Last night I was aroused by little Eddie's crying. I called and said, "What is the matter Eddie?" and he said "O Mamma! I am so hungry." and Lucy, Edward, your darling Lucy; she never complains, but she is growing thinner and thinner every day. And before God, Edward, unless you come home, we must die.
>
> Your Mary.[104]

Edward deserted, and so did hundreds and thousands of others who received similar letters that last winter of the war. General Lee in February 1865 wrote Governor Vance that despondent letters were severely weakening his army, and asked him to try to get influential citizens to "cheer the spirits of the people." But it was too late.[105]

Failure of the Confederacy to alleviate the suffering of soldiers' families may have contributed more to Southern defeat than any other single factor. Suffering, inevitable though it was, could have been lessened by better utilization of the Confederacy's resources and by more equitable treatment of the poor. One especially flagrant injustice, which caused enormous protest by the poor, was the law exempting the owners of twenty or more slaves, while permitting no exemption on the basis of white dependents.

The amazing thing is not the number of poor women who lost heart and beseeched their husbands to return home, but rather that so many endured their hardship with little or no complaint and that some had enough character and spiritual stamina to write encouraging letters to loved ones in the army. Colonel James C. Nisbet, who commanded a regiment of Georgians made up in large part of soldiers from lowly homes wrote after the war:

> It was upon the women that the greatest burden of this horrid war fell. . . . While the men were carried away with the drunkenness of the war, she dwelt in the stillness of her desolate home. . . . May the movement to erect monuments in every Southern State to our heroic Southern women carve in marble a memorial to her cross and passion.[106]

Nisbet's tribute was well deserved. However, the monuments standing in the town squares throughout the South today are not to the heroic women, but rather to the men whom they sent to war in 1861 and whom they sustained, with their labor and their prayers.[107] Theirs was certainly the greater sacrifice and to them should be accorded far more honor than they have yet received.

What effect, if any, did the Civil War have on the status of women? It did not transform the South into a matriarchy, as John Andrews Rice half-jokingly stated in his book, *I Came Out of the Eighteenth Century*.[108] But as Anne Scott has shown in *The Southern Lady: From Pedestal to Politics, 1830-1930*, the war and Reconstruction did weaken the patriarchy.[109] The Southern male, whose dominance both sexes accepted in antebellum times, lost caste by suffering defeat in the war he made and conducted. When he came home from that war, he could not logically regard as inferior the woman who had successfully managed farm or plantation during his absence. The sensible thing to do was for husband and wife to pool their judgments and energies in an effort to cope with the enormous problems of Reconstruction. And this is what many of them actually did. Men were slow to recognize women's changing status, as witness their opposition to granting them suffrage and admitting them to the medical profession. But women did forge ahead. The fact that they made far more progress in the forty-nine years between 1865 and World War I than in the seventy-eight years from the Revolution to 1861, as Mary Elizabeth Massey points out in *Bonnet Brigades*, shows that "the Civil War provided a springboard from which they leaped beyond the circumscribed 'woman's sphere' into that heretofore reserved for men."[110]

Notes

Chapter 1

[1]Ben Ames Williams, ed., *A Diary from Dixie* (Boston, 1949), p. x.
[2]Ben Ames Williams, *Reader's Guide to House Divided* (Boston, 1947), p. 13.
[3]Douglas S. Freeman, *The South to Posterity* (New York, 1939), p. 123.
[4]L. H. Butterfield to Bell I. Wiley, July 15, 1969.
[5]James Chesnut to Mary Boykin Miller, May 9, June 28, 1839. MSS., South Caroliniana Library, University of South Carolina.
[6]Mary B. Chesnut to Varina Howell Davis, June 15, 1883. MS., Confederate Museum, Richmond.
[7]For a discussion of the bearing of a feeling of guilt about slavery on Confederate contentiousness, see Bell I. Wiley, *The Road to Appomattox* (Memphis, 1956), pp. 102-105.
[8]Manuscript copies of Mrs. Chesnut's will are on deposit in the South Caroliniana Library.

Chapter 2

[1]Ada Sterling, ed., *A Belle of the Fifties: Memoirs of Mrs. Clay of Alabama* (New York, 1904), p. 26.

[2]Ibid., pp. 9-10.

[3]Virginia Clay to Mr. and Mrs. C. C. Clay, Sr., November 15, 1865. MS., Duke University. Unless otherwise noted, all quotations of Virginia's correspondence in this chapter are from the Clay manuscripts at Duke University.

[4]C. C. Clay, Jr., to J. W. Clay, December 20, 1842. MS., Duke University.

[5]C. C. Clay, Jr., to his father, February 3, 1843.

[6]Sterling, *A Belle of the Fifties*, p. 18.

[7]Virginia Clay to Mrs. C. C. Clay, Sr., December 1844.

[8]C. C. Clay, Jr., to his wife, March 8, 20, 1846.

[9]Virginia Clay to her husband, June 10, 20, 1852.

[10]Ibid., July 25, 1852.

[11]Ibid., October 4, 1852.

[12]Sterling, *A Belle of the Fifties*, p. 22.

[13]Ibid., p. 24.

[14]Ibid., p. 29.

[15]Ibid., p. 69.

[16]Ibid., pp. 44-45.

[17]Ibid., p. 47.

[18]Ibid., pp. 131-134.

[19]Virginia Clay to her husband, September 16, 1856.

[20]Virginia Clay to C. C. Clay, Sr., December 25, 1855.

[21]Sterling, *A Belle of the Fifties*, p. 136.

[22]Ibid., pp. 142-143.

[23]Ibid., p. 86.

[24]Huntsville, Alabama, *Democrat*, December 5, 1860, quoted in Ruth K. Nuermberger, *The Clays of Alabama* (Lexington, Ky., 1958), p. 182; Jefferson Davis to C. C. Clay, Jr., January 19, 1861. MS., Duke University.

[25]James G. Randall and David Donald, *The Divided Union* (Boston, 1961), p. 148.

[26]Ada Sterling, *A Belle of the Fifties*, p. 142.

[27]Varina Davis to Virginia Clay, May 10, 1861. MS., Duke University.

[28]Virginia Clay to Celeste Clay, July 14, 1861.

[29]Virginia Clay to Hugh L. Clay, July 28, 1861.

[30]Diary of Mary B. Chesnut, February 5, 1864. MS., South Caroliniana Library.

[31]Sterling, *A Belle of the Fifties*, p. 175.

[32]Mrs. C. C. Clay, Sr., to C. C. Clay, Jr., September 5, 1863. MS, Duke University.

[33]E. L. Autrey to C. C. Clay, Jr., February 2, 1864. MS., Duke University.

[34]C. C. Clay, Jr., to his wife, May 29, 1862.

[35]Virginia Clay to her husband, January 13, 1863, and to C. C. Clay, Sr., and his wife, January 14, 1863.

[36]Virginia Clay to her husband, February 24, 1863.

[37]Ibid., January 22, 1863.

[38]Ibid., February 14, 1863.

[39]Virginia Clay to her husband, March 6, 1863, and C. C. Clay, Jr., to his wife, March 12, 19, 1863.

[40]Virginia Clay to her husband, March 19, 1863.

[41]Ibid.

[42]C. C. Clay, Jr., to his wife, March 12, 20, 1863.

[43]C. C. Clay to W. L. Yancey, May 2, 1863. MS., Alabama Archives, Montgomery. See also Nuermberger, *The Clays of Alabama*, pp. 207-208.

[44]For a discussion of Clay's career in the Confederate Senate, see Nuermberger, *The Clays of Alabama*, pp. 183-233, and the Clay correspondence for this period in the Duke University Library.

[45]Virginia Clay to her husband, November 18, 1864.

[46]Ibid. The Clay Papers at Duke contain a list, in Clay's handwriting, of the items requested by his wife.

[47]Diary of Virginia Clay, May 16, 18. Typescript, Duke University.

[48]Ibid., May 23, 1864.

[49]R. S. Haldeman to Virginia Clay, July 24, 1865. MS., Duke University.

[50]The quotation is from the draft of Virginia Clay's letter to President Johnson in the Clay Papers at Duke University.

[51]Ben Green to Virginia Clay, October 21, 1865. MS., Duke University.

[52]Quoted in Sterling, *A Belle of the Fifties*, p. 317.

[53]Virginia Clay to her husband and to her parents-in-law, December 10, 1865.

[54]Virginia Clay to Andrew Johnson, January 11, 1866. MS. (copy), Duke University.

[55]Huntsville, Alabama, *Independent*, May 1, 1866.

[56]C. C. Clay, Jr., to his wife, November 16, 1868.

[57]Jefferson Davis to Virginia Clay, June 15, 1882. MS., Duke University.

[58]Virginia Clay to her husband, May 10, 1871.

[59]Ibid., November 11, 1868.

[60]Nuermberger, *The Clays of Alabama*, p. 318.

[61]Virginia Clay to her husband, July 25, 1852.

[62]Virginia Clay to Thomas T. Tunstall, December 10, 1856.

[63]Sterling, *A Belle of the Fifties*, p. 84.

[64]Virginia Clay to Thomas T. Tunstall, October 18, 1856.

[65]Diary of Virginia Clay, January 2, 1865.

[66]Sterling, *A Belle of the Fifties*, p. 21.

[67]Ibid., p. 119.

[68]Diary of Mary Chesnut, long entry covering period August 2-October 27, 1863. MS., South Caroliniana Library.

[69]Mrs. Roger A. Pryor, *Reminiscences of Peace and War* (New York, 1904), p. 81.

Chapter 3

[1]R. A. Howell to Mrs. W. B. Howell, November 21, 1836. MS., Mississippi Archives.

[2]Varina Davis to her mother, April 1850. MS., University of Alabama. Varina Davis, *Jefferson Davis, Ex-President of the Confederate States of America: A Memoir by His Wife* (New York, 1890), I, 188-190. Cited hereafter as Varina Davis, *Memoir*.

[3]Varina Davis, *Memoir*, I, 191-192.

[4]The Davis letters used in this study are in the library of the University

of Alabama at Tuscaloosa. Some of them are published in Hudson Strodes, ed., *Jefferson Davis: Private Letters, 1823-1889* (New York, 1966). Unless otherwise indicated, all quotations of Davis correspondence in this chapter are from the manuscript Davis letters at the University of Alabama.

[5]Varina Davis, *Memoir*, I, 200.

[6]Jefferson Davis to Mrs. W. B. Howell, April 25, 1845.

[7]Varina Davis to her mother, November 21, 1845.

[8]Ibid., January 30, April 3, 1846.

[9]Ibid., June 6, 1846.

[10]Jefferson Davis to his wife, February 25, 1847.

[11]Varina Davis to her mother, undated but summer of 1847.

[12]Varina Davis to her husband, January 24, 1849.

[13]Varina Davis, *Memoir*, I, 414.

[14]Varina Davis to her mother, January 6, May 20, 1850.

[15]Varina Davis to her husband, January 25, 1849.

[16]Mrs. W. B. Howell to her husband, October 29, 1854.

[17]Varina Davis to her mother, January 31, 1857.

[18]Ibid., January 1854.

[19]Ibid., December 16, 1857.

[20]W. A. Evans, *Jefferson Davis, His Diseases and His Doctors and a Biographical Sketch of Dr. Ewing Fox Howard* (Aberdeen, Miss., 1942), p. 7.

[21]Varina Davis to her mother, November 21, 1858, and to her husband, April 10, 1859.

[22]Varina Davis to her husband, April 18, 1859.

[23]Varina Davis to her mother, May 1859, and to her husband, July 2, 1859.

[24]Varina Davis to her parents, September 15, 1856.

[25]Howard K. Beale, ed., *The Diary of Gideon Welles* (New York, 1960), II, 255.

[26]Varina Davis, *Memoir,* I, 698-699.

[27]Jefferson Davis to Franklin Pierce, January 20, 1861, quoted in Robert McElroy, *Jefferson Davis: The Real and the Unreal* (New York, 1937), I, 255.

[28]Varina Davis, *Memoir*, II, 34-37.

[29]William Howard Russell, *My Diary North and South* (Boston, 1863), p. 177.

[30]Varina Davis to her mother, June 1861.

[31]R.F.W. Allston to his wife, July 15, 1861, in J. H. Easterby, ed., *The South Carolina Rice Plantation As Revealed in the Papers of R.F.W. Allston* (Chicago, 1945), p. 178.

[32]For the Johnston-Davis correspondence and a discussion of the controversy, see Gilbert E. Govan and James W. Livingood, *A Different Valor: The Story of General Joseph E. Johnston, C.S.A.* (Indianapolis, 1956), pp. 32, 67-69.

[33]Ibid., p. 70.

[34]Alvy L. King, *Louis T. Wigfall: Southern Fire-Eater* (Baton Rouge, 1970), p. 134.

[35]Louis T. Wigfall to C. C. Clay, Jr., August 13, 1863. MS., Duke University.

[36]Henry A. Wise to Dr. A.Y.P. Garnett, November 17, 26, 1863. MSS., Virginia Historical Society.

[37]Diary of Mary B. Chesnut, August 8, 1861. MS., South Caroliniana Library. The quotation is from the postwar revision. The original wartime version, dated August 12, states: "Mrs. Davis is beginning to find the troubles about Davis—pitched into Cobb at once."

[38]J. B. Jones, *A Rebel War Clerk's Diary* (Philadelphia, 1866), I, 111.

[39]J. R. McLean to his wife, February 23, 1862. MS., Henry E. Huntington Library.

[40]For a discussion of opposition to Davis in Congress and elsewhere, see Bell I. Wiley, *The Road to Appomattox* (Memphis, 1956), pp. 20-36.

[41]Varina Davis, *Memoir*, II, 160-163.

[42]Diary of Catherine Devereux Edmonston, May 13, 20, 1862. MS., North Carolina Archives, Raleigh. For the Richmond *Examiner*'s criticism for "standing in a corner telling his beads . . . instead of mounting his horse and putting forth every power of the Government to defeat the enemy," see editorial of May 19 quoted in Frederick S. Daniel, *The Richmond Examiner During the War* (New York, 1868), p. 54.

[43]Varina Davis, *Memoir*, II, 495. Ishbel Ross, *First Lady of the South: The Life of Mrs. Jefferson Davis* (New York, 1958), p. 177.

[44]Jefferson Davis to his wife, December 15, 1862. MS., Confederate Museum, Richmond.

[45]Diary of Mary B. Chesnut, long entry summarizing period of August 2, 1862-October 27, 1863. MS., South Caroliniana Library.

[46]Ibid.

[47]Mrs. Joseph E. Johnston to Mrs. Louis T. Wigfall, August 2, 1863, MS., Library of Congress.

[48]Diary of Mary B. Chesnut, November 30, 1863. MS., South Caroliniana Library.

[49]Richmond *Whig*, January 1, 2, 1864.

[50]Diary of Mary B. Chesnut, December 14, 1863, and subsequent entries, late 1863 and early 1864, especially that of February 12, 1864. MS., South Caroliniana Library.

[51]Richmond *Sentinel*, May 31, 1864.

[52]Varina Davis, *Memoir*, II. 497.

[53]Diary of Mary B. Chesnut, October 8, 1864. MS., South Caroliniana Library.

[54]Ibid., November 20, 1864.

[55]Varina Davis, "Christmas in the Confederate White House," New York *Sunday World Magazine*, December 13, 1896.

[56]Mrs. H. L. Clay to her sisters Jenny and Loula, January 17, 1865. MS. among C. C. Clay letters, "Confederate Notables" file, National Archives.

[57]Louis T. Wigfall to Joseph E. Johnston, February 29, 1865. MS., Henry E. Huntington Library.

[58]Edward A. Pollard, *Life of Jefferson Davis, With a Secret History of the Southern Confederacy Gathered Behind the Scenes in Richmond* (Philadelphia, 1869), pp. 436-437.

[59]Varina Davis, *Memoir*, II, 575.

[60]Richmond *Whig*, February 18, 1864, quoting correspondent of London *Herald*.

[61]William W. Blackford, *War Years with Jeb. Stuart* (New York, 1945), pp. 15-16.

[62]T. C. DeLeon, *Belles, Beaux and Brains of the Sixties* (New York, 1907), pp. 67-68.

[63]Pollard, *Life of Jefferson Davis*, p. 157.

⁶⁴DeLeon, *Belles, Beaux and Brains of the Sixties*, p. 67.

⁶⁵Varina Davis to Frances Lawley, June 8, 1898. Typescript in Pierce Butler Papers, Tulane University.

⁶⁶Varina Davis to John S. Preston, April 1, 1865. MS., Confederate Museum, Richmond.

⁶⁷Dunbar Rowland, ed., *Jefferson Davis, Constitutionalist: His Letters, Papers, and Speeches* (Jackson, Miss., 1923), VI, 539.

⁶⁸Varina Davis, *Memoir*, II, 648.

⁶⁹Varina Davis to her husband, November 13, 1865, and January 22, 1866.

⁷⁰Ibid., March 18, April 14, 1866.

⁷¹Quoted in Ross, *First Lady of the South*, p. 279.

⁷²Varina Davis, *Memoir*, II, 759-770.

⁷³Ibid., 799.

⁷⁴Varina Davis to Howell Cobb, July 6, 1868, in U. B. Phillips, ed., "The Correspondence of Robert Toombs, Alexander Stephens, and Howell Cobb," American Historical Association, *Annual Report for 1911* (Washington, D.C., 1913), II, 699.

⁷⁵Varina Davis to her husband, October 2, 1869.

⁷⁶Ibid., March 28, 1870.

⁷⁷Ibid., September 9, 1877.

⁷⁸Ibid., April 18, 1878. MS., Tulane University.

⁷⁹Quoted in Ross, *First Lady of the South*, p. 351.

⁸⁰Varina Davis, *Memoir*, II, 392.

⁸¹Ross, *First Lady of the South*, pp. 383-384.

⁸²Ibid., p. 402.

⁸³John W. Burgess, *Reminiscences of an American Scholar: The Beginning of Columbia University* (New York, 1934), p. 292.

⁸⁴Quoted in Ross, *First Lady of the South*, pp. 402-402.

⁸⁵Ibid., pp. 416-418.

Chapter 4: This chapter is based on Dr. Wiley's article in *American History Illustrated*, published by The National Historical Society, Gettysburg, Pa.

¹Quoted in Henry E. Sterkx, *Partners in Rebellion: Alabama Women in the Civil War* (Cranbury, N.J., 1970), p. 73.

[2]George A. Sala, *My Diary in America in the Midst of War* (London, 1865), II, 358.

[3]Quoted in S. F. Tenney to Alice Toomer, March 12, 1862. E. B. Duffee, Jr., ed., "War Letters of S. F. Tenney, a Soldier of the Third Georgia Regiment," *Georgia Historical Quarterly* 57 (Summer 1973):283.

[4]Diary of Betty Herndon Maury, June 3, 1861. MS., Library of Congress.

[5]J. W. Silver, ed., *A Life for the Confederacy: As Recorded in the Pocket Diaries of Pvt. Robert A. Moore* (Jackson, Tenn., 1959), pp. 29-33.

[6]Sterkx, *Partners in Rebellion*, pp. 41-43.

[7]Mrs. Susan Lear to Governor John Letcher, April 23, 1861. MS., Virginia State Library.

[8]Bell I. Wiley, *Embattled Confederates: An Illustrated History of Southerners at War* (New York, 1964), p. 163.

[9]Ibid.

[10]Sandusky, Ohio, *Register*, December 12, 1864.

[11]James I. Robertson, ed., *A Confederate Girl's Diary*, by Sarah Morgan Dawson (Bloomington, Ind., 1960), pp. 24-25.

[12]Diary of Mary B. Chesnut, August 29, 1861. MS., South Caroliniana Library.

[13]Wiley, *Embattled Confederates*, pp. 164-165.

[14]Mary Elizabeth Massey, *Bonnet Brigades: American Women and the Civil War* (New York, 1966), pp. 102-103.

[15]Wiley, *Embattled Confederates*, pp. 168-169.

[16]Ibid.

[17]Mrs. Thomas Taylor and others, eds., *South Carolina Women in the Confederacy* (Columbia, S.C., 1903-1907), I, 361.

[18]Ibid., II, 181.

[19]Diary of Mrs. Edwin H. Fay, July 26, 1863. MS., University of Texas.

[20]Clarence Poe, ed., *True Tales of the South at War: How Soldiers Fought and Families Lived, 1861-1865* (Chapel Hill, N.C., 1961), pp. 59-60.

[21]R. E. Lee to his wife, November 1, 1863. MS., Library of Congress.

[22]For Mrs. Allston's experiences, see Easterby, *The South Carolina*

Rice Plantation As Revealed in the Papers of R.F.W. Allston, pp. 198-200.

²³Wiley, *Embattled Confederates*, p. 170.

²⁴Mrs. W. W. Boyce to her husband, April 12, 1862. MS. in private possession.

²⁵C. Franklin to T. A. Harris, November 30, 1863. MS., Duke University.

²⁶Eliza J. Mountcastle to an unidentified Confederate colonel. MS., Henry E. Huntington Library.

²⁷Charles W. Wills, *Army Life of an Illinois Soldier* (Washington, D.C., 1906), p. 136.

²⁸Harvey Reid to his homefolk, December 14, 1864. MS., Wisconsin Historical Society.

²⁹M. S. Schroyer, "Company G History [147th Pa. Regt.]," *Snyder County Historical Bulletin* (Middleburg, Pa., 1939), II, 145.

³⁰Delos W. Lake to his homefolk, March 12, March 30, and April 1, 1865. MSS., Henry E. Huntington Library.

³¹John Hope Franklin, ed., *The Diary of James T. Ayers* (Springfield, Ill., 1947), p. 93.

³²For example, a court martial at Burnt Hickory, Georgia, May 31, 1864, found Privates Chas. Billingsley and William Cutsinger of the Seventh Indiana Battery guilty of raping Mrs. Louisa Smith on the night of May 28, 1864. MS., Court Martial Proceedings, National Archives.

³³Quoted in Mary Elizabeth Massey, *Refugee Life in the Confederacy* (Baton Rouge, 1964), p. 127.

³⁴Mrs. D. P. Porter to husband, November 8, 1863. MS., Mississippi Archives.

³⁵Betsy Swint Underwood, ed., "War Seen Through a Teen-Ager's Eyes," *Tennessee Historical Quarterly* 20 (1961) :181.

³⁶Quoted in Lynwood Holland, *Pierce M. B. Young* (Athens, Ga., 1964), p. 84.

³⁷Orion A. Bartholomew to his mother, January 18, 1862. MS., Indiana State Library.

³⁸Harold A. Small, ed., *The Road to Richmond: The Civil War Memoirs of Major Abner Small* (Berkeley, Calif., 1939), p. 157.

³⁹*War of the Rebellion: Official Records of the Union and Confederate*

Armies (Washington, D.C., 1880-1901), Series 1, XII, part 1, p. 617. Cited hereafter as *O.R.*

⁴⁰William H. Parkinson to his homefolk, July 27, 1862. MS. in private possession.

⁴¹Theodore C. Blegen, ed., *The Civil War Letters of Colonel Hans Christian Heg* (Northfield, Minn., 1936), p. 63.

⁰Ibid., p. 211.

⁴³Excerpts from the Journal of Margaret Dailey, December 20, 1863. Typescript in private possession.

⁴⁴Diary of Miss Susan R. Jervey, February 27, 1865, in *Two Diaries from Middle St. John's Berkeley, South Carolina, February-May, 1865* (Charleston, S.C., 1921), p. 7.

⁴⁵Mrs. Fannie A. Morrow to her sister, July 13, 1863. Typescript, University of Texas. A. P. Aldrich to J. H. Hammond, May 3, 1864. MS., Library of Congress.

⁴⁶Wiley, *Embattled Confederates*, p. 182. *Confederate Veteran* (Nashville, Tenn.), XVIII (October 1910), p. 471.

⁴⁷Wiley, *Embattled Confederates*, p. 183.

⁴⁸Anne F. Scott, *The Southern Lady: From Pedestal to Politics, 1830-1930* (Chicago, 1970), p. 86.

⁴⁹Daniel E. Huger Smith and others, eds., *Mason Smith Family Letters, 1860-1868* (Columbia, S.C., 1950), pp. 96-197.

⁵⁰Mrs. S.P.H. Drake to her son, December 11, 1864. Typescript in private possession.

⁵¹Georgia Smith to Mrs. W. A. Couper, n.d., but December 1862. MS., University of North Carolina.

⁵²Wiley, *Embattled Confederates*, pp. 194-196.

⁵³Ibid., pp. 197-199.

⁵⁴W. J. Mims to his wife, June 6, 1863. MS. in private possession.

⁵⁵Wirt A. Cate, ed., *Two Soldiers: The Campaign Diaries of Thomas J. Key and Robert J. Campbell* (Chapel Hill, N.C., 1938), pp. 20-21.

⁵⁶William L. Nugent to his wife, March 27, 1864. MS. in private possession.

⁵⁷Orville C. Bumpass to his wife, October 22, 1864. MS., Evans Memorial Library, Aberdeen, Mississippi.

⁵⁸Richmond *Enquirer*, August 22, 1864.

[59]Bell I. Wiley, *The Life of Johnny Reb: The Common Soldier of the Confederacy* (Indianapolis, 1943), p. 53.

[60]Mrs. E. Jett to her husband, September 2, 1864. MS. in private possession.

[61]For a discussion of the experiences and attitudes of the slaves during the Civil War, see Bell I. Wiley, *Southern Negroes, 1861-1865* (New Haven, 1938), pp. 1-172.

[62]Diary of Betty H. Maury, May 16, 1862. MS., Library of Congress.

[63]*Memoirs of General William T. Sherman* (Bloomington, Ind., 1957), II, 180.

[64]Wiley, *Southern Negroes*, p. 19.

[65]See George P. Rawick, ed., *The American Slave* (Westport, Conn., 1972), Vols. I-XIX.

[66]Ibid., XII, 258.

[67]S. S. Champion to his wife, n.d., but May 1863. MS in private possession.

[68]*O.R.*, Series 1, XLVII, part 2, p. 33.

[69]Diary of Richard H. Mockett, January 1, 1865. MS., University of Michigan.

[70]Sallie McGough to Mrs. John B. Evans, July 19, 1864. MS., Duke University.

[71]Bell I. Wiley, *The Plain People of the Confederacy* (Baton Rouge, 1943), p. 60.

[72]Lezinka White to Bettie Stuart, March 3, 1865. MS., Mississippi Archives.

[73]Diary of Virginia French, May 26, 1862. Typescript, Tennessee State Library.

[74]*Johnson's Common School Arithmetic* (Raleigh, N.C., 1864), p. 38. M. B. Moore, *Primary Geography Arranged As a Reading Book for Common Schools* (Raleigh, N.C., 1864), p. 47.

[75]Mrs. Thomas Taylor and others, eds., *South Carolina Women in the Confederacy*, II, 32.

[76]Elizabeth W. Allston Pringle, *Chronicles of Chicora Wood* (New York, 1922), pp. 177-179.

[77]Lucy Stinnette to "Dear Laura," March 1, 1864. MS., University of Texas.

[78]Fannie Baylor to Virginia King, March 23, 1863. MS., University of North Carolina.

[79]Mrs. J. G. Ramsay to her husband, November 18, 1864. MS. University of North Carolina.

[80]The Journal of Catherine D. Edmonston, various entries, January 1862-March 1865.

[81]Anderson, *Brokenburn*, p. 87.

[82]Mrs. Ella Harper to her husband, May 30, 1862. MS., University of North Carolina.

[83]Ibid., July 15, 1862. MS., University of North Carolina.

[84]The Peddy letters are in the Emory University Library.

[85]Sallie Lovett to her husband, February 14, 1864. MS., Emory University.

[86]Mrs. John Dorsey to her husband, April 22, 1864. MS. in private possession.

[87]For example, Mrs. V. L. Brooke wrote Mrs. R.M.T. Hunter, March 21, 1861: "My baby is only eleven months old and *nurses* entirely, and I intend *to nurse her always*. If I thought such a thing could happen to me again, I really think suicide would be justifiable—certainly preferable." MS., University of Virginia.

[88]Brigadier General Dorsey Pender to his wife, March 6, 1862. MS., University of North Carolina.

[89]Mrs. Braxton Bragg to her husband, October 13, 1861. MS., University of Texas.

[90]Ibid., October 16, 1862. Quoted in Grady McWhiney, *Braxton Bragg and Confederate Defeat* (New York, 1969), I, 324-325.

[91]Mrs. Braxton Bragg to her husband, September 28, 1863. MS., University of Texas.

[92]Augusta Evans to J.L.M. Curry, various dates, especially July 15, 1863. MS., Library of Congress. For relationships between Augusta Evans and Beauregard, see T. Harry Williams, *Beauregard: Napoleon in Gray* (Baton Rouge, 1954), pp. 160, 171, and 199.

[93]Mrs. Howell Cobb to her husband, August 30, 1865. MS., University of Georgia.

[94]Mrs. J. G. Ramsay to her husband, November 18, 1864. MS., University of North Carolina.

[95]Mrs. John C. Breckinridge to her husband, April 13, 1863. MS., National Archives.

[96]Troup Butler to his wife, March 24, 1862. MS. in private possession.

[97]William H. Ivey to his wife, March 5, 1863. MS. in private possession.

[98]Alfred W. Bell to his wife, September 5, 23, 1863. MS., Duke University.

[99]Sallie McGough to Mrs. John B. Evans, July 19, 1864. MS., Duke University.

[100]Robert Partin, ed., "The Wartime Experiences of Margaret McCalla: Confederate Refugee from East Tennessee," *Tennessee Historical Quarterly* XXIV(Spring 1965): 39-53.

[101]Mrs. J.B. Jett to her husband, June 12, 1864, and various subsequent dates until December 1864. MS. in private possession.

[102]Mrs. W. A. Hamner to her husband, November 20, 1864. MS., University of Virginia.

[103]"A Poor Woman and Children" to Governor Zebulon B. Vance, January 10, 1865. MS., North Carolina Archives.

[104]Quoted in Ella Lonn, *Desertion During the Civil War* (New York, 1928), p. 13.

[105]*O.R.*, Series 1, XLVII, part 2, p. 1270.

[106]Bell I. Wiley, ed., *Four Years on the Firing Line*, by J.C. Nisbet (Jackson, Tenn., 1963), p. 170.

[107]An exception is the Confederate monument in Greenwood, Mississippi, on which is inscribed: "To the Confederate Woman . . . whose heart and life were a sacrifice, offered as valiantly and unselfishly upon the altar of her southland as was any warrior's life upon the battlefield. So to her in part we have placed this monument, that all may know she loved her country, and enfold her memory in eternal glory, cherishing it forever."

[108]John A. Rice, *I Came Out of the Eighteenth Century* (New York, 1942), p. 116.

[109]Scott, *The Southern Lady*, pp. 96-102.

[110]Massey, *Bonnet Brigades*, p. 367.

Bibliographical Note

This study of Confederate women is based mainly on the manuscript letters and diaries of the women themselves.

The chapter on Mrs. Chesnut is based primarily on her handwritten diary on deposit in the South Caroliniana Library of the University of South Carolina. The various versions of the manuscript are discussed in Chapter 1. As stated there, only a very small portion of the journal—that covering the period from November 11, 1860 to October 1, 1861—is the original account that Mrs. Chesnut wrote during the war. The entries that she made during the conflict for the period after October 1, 1861, were either lost or destroyed. The great bulk of the extant manuscript was written by Mrs. Chesnut in the 1880s and was based on remnants of the original, on random notes made during and after the war, and on recollections. This rewrite, as noted in Chapter 1, is the basis for both the Martin-Avary and Ben Ames Williams editions of the diary published respectively in 1905 and 1949. It is more of a journal-memoir than a diary. Even so, it is a remarkably fine record of the wartime experiences and observations of a perceptive and highly articulate lady who moved freely among leading Confederates of both sexes.

Mrs. Chesnut's letters are very rare. A few prewar and postwar letters are preserved in the South Caroliniana Library, the South Carolina Historical Society, the Museum of the Confederacy, and the Wisconsin State Historical Society. The South Caroliniana Library also has a manuscript, "A Boarding School Fifty Years Ago," written by Mrs. Chesnut after the war telling of her girlhood experiences in Madame Talvande's school in Charleston.

From the Baker Memorial Library of Dartmouth College I obtained a Xerox copy of the typescript used by Ben Ames Williams in preparing his 1949 edition of *A Diary from Dixie*. Williams' marks and jottings on this typescript were very helpful in determining the nature and extent of his editorial work. As previously stated, Williams' editing consisted largely in eliminating repetitious and quoted material and refining Mrs. Chesnut's sometimes choppy narrative. While the basis of his edition, as noted in Chapter 1, was Mrs. Chesnut's postwar revision, he inserted a few sentences from the three original volumes, but not those telling of the estrangement from Mrs. Davis in the summer of 1861. His reasons for excluding these passages were probably that the quarrel was shortlived and untypical, and that Mrs. Chesnut herself chose to omit all references to it when she rewrote the account in the 1880s. He also left out some disparaging comments about Jews.

The basic source for the chapter on Mrs. Clay was the large collection of Clay letters at Duke University. Some information was gleaned from Mrs. Clay's memoir, *A Belle of the Fifties*, edited by Ada Sterling (New York, 1904). Helpful information on Mrs. Clay, her family, her friends, and the times in which she lived was obtained from Ruth Ketring Nuermberger's excellent study, *The Clays of Alabama: A Planter-Lawyer-Politician Family* (Lexington, Kentucky, 1958).

The best collection of Varina Howell Davis letters is at the University of Alabama. Most of these letters were published in *Jefferson Davis: Private Letters, 1823-1889*, edited by Hudson Strode (New York, 1966). The published letters should be used with great care because the editor deleted words, sentences, and paragraphs without inserting marks of ellipsis. In his introduction to the volume, the editor states that he has omitted these marks "for the reader's convenience"; he characterizes the deletions as "long, gossipy paragraphs about persons of no continuous significance in the Davis's lives, as well as routine reports on the health of herself, her children, relatives and acquaintances." A reader seeking a thorough understanding of a person as complex as Varina Howell Davis may want to see and evaluate for himself what Mr. Strode construed as gossipy and routine. A few of Mrs. Davis's letters are available in the manuscript holdings of the Museum of the Confederacy, Tulane University, Transylvania University, and Rice University. All the Davis correspondence quoted in this study is from manuscript sources.

Mrs. Davis's memoir, *Jefferson Davis: Ex-President of the Confederate States* (2 volumes, New York, 1890), while uncritical and concerned primarily with the career of her husband, provides valuable insights into her attitudes and activities. The only good biography of Mrs. Davis is Ishbel Ross, *First Lady of the South* (New York, 1958); it is a well-researched, perceptive, and attractively written study.

For Confederate women in general manuscript sources are abundant, though scattered. The best collections are at the University of North Carolina, Duke, the University of Texas, Tulane, and the University of South Carolina. Other depositories with substantial holdings include Emory University, the Tennessee State Library, the South Carolina Historical Society, the Mississippi State Department of Archives and History, Louisiana State University, the North Carolina Department of Archives and History, the Virginia Historical Society, and the University of Georgia.

Very few women of the yeoman classes kept diaries, but many of them wrote letters to relatives and friends in Confederate service. Soldier recipients often destroyed these letters because of the inconvenience of keeping them or the fear that they might fall into the hands of the Yankees. Still, enough of them have survived to provide a fairly full view of the character and experiences of the Confederacy's lower class women. This is not true of the blacks, who were barred by state law from learning to read and write.

Many diaries and memoirs of upper class women have been published. Among the most informative of these are: *The Journal of Catherine Devereaux Edmonston, 1800-1866*, edited by Margaret M. Jones (privately printed, 1954); *Brokenburn: The Journal of Kate Stone, 1861-1868*, edited by John Q. Anderson (Baton Rouge, 1955); Elizabeth Allston Pringle, *The Chronicles of Chicora Wood* (New York, 1923); Elizabeth Allen Coxe, *Memories of a South Carolina Plantation* (privately printed, 1912); Parthenia Hague, *A Blockaded Family: Life in Southern Alabama during the Civil War* (Boston, 1888); Susan D. Smedes, *Memorials of a Southern Planter* (New York, 1900); Eliza Frances Andrews, *The War-Time Journal of a Georgia Girl*, edited by Spencer B. King, Jr. (Macon, Georgia, 1960); Sarah Morgan Dawson, *A Confederate Girl's Diary*, edited by James I. Robertson (Bloomington, Indiana, 1960); *The Diary of Dolly Lunt Burge*, edited by James I.

Robertson (Athens, Georgia, 1962); *Kate: The Journal of a Confederate Nurse*, edited by Richard B. Harwell (Baton Rouge, 1959); Cornelia P. McDonald, *A Diary With Reminiscences of the War and Refugee Life in the Shenandoah Valley* (Nashville, 1934); Phoebe Yates Pember, *A Southern Woman's Story*, edited by Bell I. Wiley (Jackson, Tennessee, 1959); Sallie A. Putnam, *Richmond during the War: Four Years of Personal Observation* (New York, 1867); *The Journal of Julia LeGrand, New Orleans, 1862-1863*, edited by Kate M. Rowland and Mrs. Morris Croxall (Richmond, 1911); Judith B. McGuire, *Diary of a Southern Refugee during the War* (New York, 1867); *The Mason Smith Family Letters*, edited by Daniel E. Huger and others (Columbia, South Carolina, 1950); Mrs. D. Giraud Wright, *A Southern Girl in '61: The War-Time Memories of a Confederate Senator's Daughter* (New York, 1905). Two useful compilations of women's narratives, edited by Katherine M. Jones, are *Heroines of Dixie: Confederate Women Tell Their Story of the War* (Indianapolis, 1955) and *When Sherman Came: Southern Women and the "Great March"* (Indianapolis, 1964). A similar, but older, collection is *The Women of the South in War Times*, compiled by Matthew Page Andrews (Baltimore, 1924).

Confederate women have been the subject of many secondary accounts and most of these emphasize the role of the upper classes. Mary Elizabeth Massey's three excellent books, *Ersatz in the Confederacy* (Columbia, South Carolina, 1952), *Refugee Life in the Confederacy* (Baton Rouge, 1964), and *Bonnet Brigades: American Women and the Civil War* (New York, 1966), are especially informative. An older but still very solid and useful work is *The Women of the Confederacy*, by Frances B. Simkins and James W. Patton (Richmond, 1936). Anne F. Scott's *The Southern Lady: From Pedestal to Politics, 1830-1930* (Chicago, 1970) contains perceptive comments on the women of the Confederacy. Among the various studies on the state level, the most recent and the best is *Partners in Rebellion: Alabama Women during the Civil War*, by H. E. Sterkx (Cranbury, New Jersey, 1970).

Index

199

204

Civil War Books
by Bell Irvin Wiley:

SOUTHERN NEGROES, 1861-1865
THE LIFE OF JOHNNY REB: THE COMMON SOLDIER OF THE
  CONFEDERACY
THE PLAIN PEOPLE OF THE CONFEDERACY
THE LIFE OF BILLY YANK: THE COMMON SOLDIER OF THE
  UNION
THE ROAD TO APPOMATTOX
THEY WHO FOUGHT HERE
EMBATTLED CONFEDERATES: AN ILLUSTRATED HISTORY OF
  SOUTHERNERS AT WAR